Hidden scandal, secret shame
Torture and ill-treatment of children

This report is one of a series of publications issued by Amnesty International as part of its worldwide campaign against torture. Other reports issued as part of the campaign, which was launched in October 2000, include: *Take a step to stamp out torture* (AI Index: ACT 40/13/00); *Broken bodies, shattered minds — Torture and ill-treatment of women* (AI Index: ACT 40/01/01); *Stopping the torture trade* (AI Index: ACT 40/02/01).

- **Take a step to stamp out torture** — join Amnesty International's campaign against torture
- Join Amnesty International and other local and international human rights organizations which fight torture
- Make a donation to support Amnesty International's work
- Tell friends and family about the campaign and ask them to join too
- Register to take action against torture at **www.stoptorture.org** and campaign online. Visitors to the website will be able to appeal on behalf of individuals at risk of torture

Cover: Children pray before lunch at a São Paulo juvenile offenders' home in Brazil. Juvenile offenders in São Paulo are forced to live in degrading and often overcrowded conditions. Ill-treatment, sometimes amounting to torture, is endemic. © Reuters/Popperfoto

Amnesty International (AI) is a worldwide movement of people who campaign for human rights. AI works towards the observance of all human rights as enshrined in the Universal Declaration of Human Rights and other international standards. It seeks to promote the observance of the full range of human rights, which it considers to be indivisible and interdependent, through campaigning and public awareness activities, as well as through human rights education and pushing for ratification and implementation of human rights treaties.

AI's work is based on careful research and on the standards agreed by the international community. AI is a voluntary, democratic, self-governing movement with more than a million members and supporters in more than 140 countries and territories. It is funded largely by its worldwide membership and by donations from the public. No funds are sought or accepted from governments for AI's work in documenting and campaigning against human rights violations.

AI is independent of any government, political persuasion or religious creed. It does not support or oppose any government or political system, nor does it support or oppose the views of the victims whose rights it seeks to protect. It is concerned solely with the impartial protection of human rights.

AI takes action against some of the gravest violations by governments of people's civil and political rights. The focus of its campaigning against human rights violations is to:

- free all prisoners of conscience. According to AI's Statute, these are people detained for their political, religious or other conscientiously held beliefs or because of their ethnic origin, sex, colour, language, national or social origin, economic status, birth or other status – who have not used or advocated violence;
- ensure fair and prompt trials for all political prisoners;
- abolish the death penalty, torture and other ill-treatment of prisoners;
- end political killings and "disappearances".

AI calls on armed political groups to respect human rights and to halt abuses such as the detention of prisoners of conscience, hostage-taking, torture and unlawful killings.

AI also seeks to support the protection of human rights by other activities, including its work with the United Nations (UN) and regional intergovernmental organizations, and its work for refugees, on international military, security and police relations, and on economic and cultural relations.

Hidden scandal, secret shame
Torture and ill-treatment of children

Amnesty International Publications

Please note that readers may find some of the photographs and case histories contained in this report disturbing.

First published in 2000 by
Amnesty International USA
322 Eighth Avenue
New York, NY 10001

www.amnestyusa.org

© Copyright
Amnesty International Publications 2000
ISBN: 1-887204-23-7
AI Index: ACT 40/38/00
Original language: English

Cover design by: Synergy

Printed by:
Globe Litho
111 Lester Street
Wallington, NJ 07057

Library of Congress Card Number: 00-193200

CONTENTS

INTRODUCTION

The fact that children could suffer torture at all should come as a terrible shock. Their dependency and vulnerability should render them immune from the atrocities adults inflict on one another. Their very innocence should put them beyond reach. Yet violence against children is endemic: children are tortured by the police or security forces; detained in appalling conditions; beaten or sexually abused by parents, teachers or employers; maimed, killed or turned into killers by war. Some are victims many times over, first of the chronic poverty and discrimination that renders them vulnerable to torture and ill-treatment, then to the injustice and impunity that allows it to continue unpunished.

© Dario Mitidieri

A child searching for food at Chowpatti Beach, Bombay, India, is approached by a policeman wielding a *lathi* (long wooden stick).

Amnesty International (AI) launched a global campaign against torture in October 2000 to raise public awareness of the extent to which torture has persisted to the eve of the 21st century. This report, released as a part of that campaign, focuses on children around the world who are the victims of torture or cruel, inhuman or degrading treatment. It will emphasize that torture and ill-treatment of children is not only a social or cultural issue, but a human rights violation, which the state has an obligation to take effective steps to prevent. The campaign seeks to galvanize people around the world to **Take a step to stamp out torture**. It focuses on three major areas: preventing torture; overcoming impunity; and confronting discrimination.

Chapter 1 of this report identifies and describes the international legal standards that define and prohibit the torture and ill-treatment of children, and attempts to explain and resolve some of the difficulties inherent in responding to the torture of children within a legal framework originally conceived for adults. Chapters 2, 3 and 4 draw on AI's field research and other direct evidence to examine the contexts in which the torture of children actually occurs. This report will also make recommendations for ending the torture of children.

Guided by the framework of the UN Convention on the Rights of the Child (the Children's Convention), AI's work to prevent the torture of children focuses on three situations: juvenile justice; children in armed conflict; and children in the community. AI's investigations within these areas concentrate on human rights violations carried out by states and on abuses by armed opposition groups, and this report similarly focuses on such incidents. It is therefore not an exhaustive survey of all forms of violence against children, and in particular, does not address violence committed by private individuals, which accounts for much of the abuse inflicted on children.

The Children's Convention is the only human rights treaty to be even close to achieving universal ratification.[1] Such widespread support confirms that there is a consensus possible with regard to the protection of children and their rights — a consensus that can pave the way for a more positive attitude towards the fundamental rights and freedoms due to all people. Enunciating and confirming children's rights is no more than a first step; we must also work to ensure that these rights are implemented. Although the Children's Convention provides a comprehensive reference point for children's rights in a broad range of situations, AI also reminds states of their obligations under other human rights standards to protect the rights of the child.[2] The Children's Convention may be the most widely ratified human rights treaty in the world, but it is still a long, long way from universal acceptance to universal observance.

1: CHILDREN AND TORTURE

ILLC NO A LA INJUSTICIA
E IMPUNIDAD DE LOS HECHOS
-NO PARTICIPA EN LA GUERRA
DIRECTA O INDIREC...NTE
NI PORTA ARMAS
-NO MANIPULA NI E...
INFORMACION...
DE LAS PAR...

ZONA NEUTRAL
SAN JOSE DE APARTADO

© Private

Children of the peace community of San José de Apartadó, Colombia. In March 1997 the community declared itself a peace community and demanded that all parties to the conflict respect the lives of the civilian population and their right not to be drawn into taking sides in the conflict.

The rights of the child

The notion of special childhood rights derives from the universal recognition that children, by reason of their physical and emotional immaturity, are dependent on their family and community and, more widely, on adult structures of political and economic power to safeguard their well-being. A series of international instruments codifies the protections and rights that children are entitled to: children have the right to be protected from all forms of physical or mental violence; from the effects of armed conflict; and from sexual and other forms of exploitation. Children's special rights include the right to an education; to play, rest and leisure; to protection from hazardous or harmful work, including military duty; and to be confined or imprisoned only in exceptional circumstances or as a last resort and for the shortest possible time.

3

Children are entitled to adult protection, but they are not adult property: children also have the right to make decisions on their own behalf in accordance with their maturity. Children have the right to be heard and to have their own opinions on matters affecting them taken into account, "in accordance with the age and maturity of the child". Very young children rely on others to express their views and protect their best interests; as they grow older, they become more able to speak for themselves and engage in decision-making on their own behalf. One of the guiding principles of the Children's Convention is that the "best interests of the child" should be a primary consideration in all decisions or procedures related to the child.

The legal definition of a "child"

A "child", according to most international legal standards, is anyone under the age of 18. Most of the world's countries have also set the legal age of majority or adulthood at 18. AI uses this definition, as do most other non-governmental organizations (NGOs) and children's rights groups. The African Charter on the Rights and Welfare of the Child says that a child is "every human being below the age of 18 years", while the Children's Convention is less categorical, saying that every human being under the age of 18 is a child, unless majority is attained earlier under national law. It appears that this exception could be used by states to justify refusing rights contained in the Children's Convention to those who do not fit the definition of children under national law — i.e. where the age of majority has been set below 18 by a particular state. However, the Committee on the Rights of the Child (see page 10) has been consistent in applying this clause to mean that definitions of majority set lower than 18 are allowed only if they do not prejudice any of the rights protected by the Children's Convention.

The term "juvenile" also appears in human rights texts, although it is not exactly interchangeable; it usually refers to those who are able to be charged and tried in the juvenile justice system. The UN's Beijing Rules[3] allow for a "wide variety of ages coming under the definition of "juvenile", ranging from seven years to 18 years or above", while the UN Rules for the Protection of Juveniles Deprived of their Liberty states that "a juvenile is every person under the age of 18", but adds that the age below which it should not be possible to deprive a child of his or her liberty should also be determined by law. In some countries, all young offenders or all those housed in youth offender institutions are referred to as juveniles, even some who may be up to 21 or even 24 years old.

Concepts which help define childhood, such as maturity, and the age of criminal responsibility, rely largely on social and cultural factors. At what age different levels of maturity are expected varies enormously from society to society — the Children's Convention is vague, intentionally so, about the age of criminal responsibility, and the principle that the child's opinions should be given due consideration is in accordance with the "maturity" of the child, rather than his or her age.

In some societies, childhood is a condition fixed by the position of the child within the community rather than his or her age. Those still under parental authority are regarded as children, no matter what their age, while those who have taken on adult roles and responsibilities are given social rights and duties accordingly. In much of the world, even small children have significant economic responsibilities: they have to work, either to support themselves or as part of the family economy, so there is little time left over for school or play. A South African activist and educator has pointed out that the conception of the child as "an individual shorn of most obligations, economically dependent, politically uninvolved, emotionally and morally immature, and secure within and represented by a family", fits the experiences of very few children in the world.[4]

Yet those children who are forced to bear the financial burdens and emotional responsibilities of adulthood are at even greater risk of abuse precisely because they are not viewed as children. It may not be recognized that they are still emotionally and physically immature, and so in need of the additional safeguards and protections provided by the relevant legal standards.

Age of criminal responsibility

The age of criminal responsibility is usually different from the age of majority; it is commonly held to be the age at which a child can be expected to know right from wrong, understand the consequences of his or her actions, and be of sufficient emotional and intellectual maturity to understand and participate in hearings, trials or other procedures within the appropriate juvenile justice setting. AI does not take a position on where the minimum age of criminal responsibility should be set, nor does the Children's Convention, although the UN's Beijing Rules recommend that it should "not be fixed at too low an age level bearing in mind the facts of emotional, mental and intellectual maturity".[5] The age of criminal responsibility varies between countries and even within them. In some countries, the age of majority and the age of criminal responsibility are both linked to puberty, often different for boys and girls. But even though most states set the age of criminal responsibility below 18, the individual is still regarded as a child and is entitled to the rights in the Children's Convention governing the child's treatment at the hands of law enforcement and judicial authorities. In some countries, the age levels set for rights and responsibilities connected to adulthood vary enormously. In the USA, for instance, 18-year-olds are regarded as responsible enough to vote, 17-year-olds can join the army, 16-year-olds can get married or be sentenced to death,[6] and 12-year-olds can work 14-hour days on farms, but only those who are 21 or over are allowed to buy wine or beer.

There is obviously no single age at which everyone makes the transition from child to adult, but 18 is the most widely recognized benchmark. It is an age at which the vast majority of young people can be thought of as young adults. By the age of 18 most young people will have completed their formal education and will be able to recognize and fulfil the social obligations and responsibilities demanded of an adult member of civil society. Most will have attained a certain level of emotional and physical development, and will be fully capable of making and implementing decisions on their own behalf.[7]

The protection of children under international law

Both torture and ill-treatment are prohibited by international human rights and humanitarian law, and almost all national law. But children are entitled to even higher levels of protection; international standards guarantee children protection from all forms of violence, whatever the reason, whoever the perpetrator. Article 19 of the Children's Convention obliges states parties to protect children from "all forms of physical or mental violence, injury or abuse, neglect or negligent treatment, maltreatment or exploitation, including sexual abuse, while in the care of parent(s), legal guardian(s) or any other person who has the care of the child."

Although AI's research on children — and this report — focuses largely on torture and ill-treatment carried out by agents of the state and by armed political groups,[8] or those acting at their instigation or with their consent or acquiescence. AI also promotes the full range of state obligations to establish and enforce laws that protect children from abuses carried out in the private sphere. AI holds that the state's responsibility to take effective steps to protect children from all forms of violence extends to domestic violence amounting to torture or ill-treatment; governments must prevent and punish torture whether inflicted by state officials or by private individuals.

The prohibition of torture in international law is absolute, non-derogable, and reiterated in a number of international treaties and instruments. It is not weakened by any reference to circumstances or statute of limitations; there is no defence of superior orders. There can be no justification, excuse, or impunity for those who commit or order acts of torture. Torturers should always be held accountable, no matter where they are, no matter who they are, no matter how much time has passed since they carried out their crimes.

Definitions of torture in international law

The definition contained in Article 1 of the UN Convention against Torture and Other Cruel, Inhuman or Degrading Treatment or Punishment (the Convention against Torture) states that: "For the purposes of this Convention, the term "torture" means any act by which severe pain or suffering, whether physical or mental, is intentionally inflicted on a person for such purposes as obtaining from him or a third person information or a confession, punishing him for an act he or a third person has committed or is suspected of having committed, or intimidating or coercing him or a third person, or for any reason based on discrimination of any kind, when such pain or suffering is inflicted by or at the instigation of or with the consent or acquiescence of a public official or other person acting in an official capacity. It does not include pain or suffering arising only from, inherent in or incidental to lawful sanctions."

Acts which do not amount to torture, but still constitute "cruel, inhuman or degrading treatment or punishment" (ill-treatment), are similarly prohibited, although the Convention against Torture does not attempt to clarify precisely what such treatment may involve. The scope of the term was clearly meant to be broad, and interpreted so as to extend the widest possible protection against physical or mental abuse.[9] There is some jurisprudence aimed at setting boundaries between torture and ill-treatment, which is important mainly in that the state has greater obligations in respect of torture, but the boundaries must remain flexible, particularly as the designation of an act as torture in a particular case may depend on the individual experience of the victim. When a victim suffers different kinds of ill-treatment at once, the cumulative effect might also constitute torture, as could be the case if ill-treatment occurs over prolonged periods.

The Inter-American Convention to Prevent and Punish Torture gives a somewhat broader definition, including as torture "the use of methods upon a person intended to obliterate the personality of the victim or to diminish his physical or mental capacities, even if they do not cause physical pain or mental anguish". The Rome Statute of the International Criminal Court, adopted in 1998 and likely to enter into force in the near future, defines the crime against humanity of torture as "the intentional infliction of severe pain or suffering, whether physical or mental, upon a person in the custody or under the control of the accused".[10] The Rome Statute does not define the war crime of torture.[11]

Two regional courts, the Inter-American Court of Human Rights and the European Court of Human Rights, have rendered judgments providing significant jurisprudence on individual cases of torture and other violations of the regional human rights treaties under which they were created,[12] although few of their cases have dealt specifically with the torture of children.

© Graham Turner/*The Guardian*

Punishment cell in a juvenile detention centre, UK. The use of solitary confinement as a disciplinary measure for juveniles is prohibited by the UN Rules for the Protection of Juveniles Deprived of their Liberty.

Convention on the Rights of the Child

The Children's Convention uses the Convention against Torture definition of torture as a starting point:[13] Article 37 of the Children's Convention forbids torture and cruel, inhuman or degrading treatment, adding that "neither capital punishment nor life imprisonment without possibility of release shall be imposed for offences committed by persons below eighteen years of age." The inclusion of these two provisions in the article on torture suggests that the framers of the Children's Convention envisaged the possibility that these could be regarded as torture for children. While not explicitly expanding the definition of torture, the Children's Convention considerably expands the physical protection due to children beyond that provided in other human rights instruments and bridges the public/private divide by placing greater obligations on the state to take actions leading to the eradication of violence in the home, school or workplace.

Implementation of the Children's Convention is monitored by the Committee on the Rights of the Child, which comprises 10 experts "of high moral standing and recognized competence in the field".[14] They are elected by secret ballot of all states parties, each of which may nominate one national expert. Because the Children's Convention is so wide-ranging, covering social policy as well as law, the Committee usually includes people from a wide variety of professional backgrounds, such as human rights and international law, juvenile justice, social work, medicine, journalism and governmental and non-governmental work. Governments are obliged to report to the Committee within two years of the treaty coming into effect in their country, specifying the steps taken to bring national laws, policy and practice into line with the principles of the Children's Convention. The Committee examines the facts and hears a wide range of evidence relevant to the government's report, often from NGOs, and meets with each government to review what it has done to implement the provisions of the Children's Convention. The Committee advises governments on the implementation of the Children's Convention, and engages them in substantive policy discussions on the resolution of specific children's rights issues. At the end of the process, the Committee adopts "concluding observations", which provide a series of recommendations on how states can improve their implementation of the provisions of the Children's Convention. Governments must submit progress reports every five years.

But the Children's Convention offers limited practical protection to the individual. It provides no enforceable right to compensation, and the Committee on the Rights of the Child has no capacity to receive or investigate individual complaints. The Convention against Torture, while setting a more restrictive definitional standard, offers greater potential for a victim seeking remedy. It provides protection to anyone against being returned to a country where they are at risk of torture; it reduces the chances of torturers finding safe havens in other countries by requiring states parties to extradite suspects or to exercise universal jurisdiction; and obliges governments to implement and enforce legislation against torture, bring torturers to justice and compensate the victims. The Committee against Torture[15] reviews periodic and special reports by states on the implementation of their anti-torture obligations, and is able to receive and investigate individual complaints, provided that the state concerned has accepted these procedures. However, the greater potential for protection offered by the Convention against Torture has to be offset by the fact that while the Children's Convention has been ratified by every country in the world except Somalia (which has had no government since 1991) and the USA, only 122 states to date are bound as states parties to respect and enforce the provisions of the Convention against Torture.[16]

The UN Special Rapporteur on torture

The Special Rapporteur on torture, established by the UN Commission on Human Rights, can make urgent appeals on behalf of anyone at imminent risk of being tortured or ill-treated.[17] He can undertake fact-finding visits to countries to obtain first-hand information and can then make recommendations on how the government can improve the situation. He issues individual reports on these countries, and also reports annually to the UN Commission on Human Rights. The Special Rapporteur can also receive allegations of torture or ill-treatment from any individual or agency.

The special situation of children

The Children's Convention prohibits torture, but does not define it. There are a number of questions around definitions of torture and ill-treatment derived from other instruments which suggest that standard legal definitions do not fully reflect the special situation of children. Under the Convention against Torture, an act of torture is understood to have a definite aim or purpose, and some form of direct or indirect involvement of state officials. The prohibition includes those acting with the "consent or acquiescence" of the state, and within this nexus the application of the Convention against Torture can be quite broadly interpreted, extending to acts committed by private individuals which the state could reasonably be expected to have prevented through effective and enforced legislation. The concept of public official is also open to broad interpretation, and can include teachers and doctors as well as police officers and prison wardens.[18] The critical element appears to be that the abuser's authority is recognized by the state, even if they are not acting on behalf of the state.[19] Yet even taking the broadest possible interpretation, the Convention against Torture still operates in a public, largely adult, domain. The definition of "torture" it provides was discussed and agreed with the situation of adults and how adults are treated in mind. It does not address the full range of the experiences of children, particularly in that it may exclude the arenas — such as private or domestic space — in which children are most likely to be abused.

Violence against girls

This aspect of the Convention definition of torture has a particular impact on how violence against girls is likely to be characterized, in that girls are more likely to suffer attack or abuse in the home than in custody, at school or a workplace. Although girls are entitled to the protection from all forms of violence guaranteed by the Children's Convention, even this wide-ranging provision does not address their double susceptibility. Girls are at increased risk of physical, sexual and psychological abuse from an early age. Preferences for boys may endanger the life of a baby girl, while culturally determined notions about the greater economic and social value of boys often means that girls suffer constant, if low level, forms of discriminatory ill-treatment, including lack of health care, inadequate food, and reduced access to education.

Girls in the public sphere may also be detained or abused for reasons to do with gender — because of their opposition to dress or behaviour codes, for instance — and once in detention are at risk of sexual torture, including rape, or sexual humiliation and harassment. The sexual harassment of street children who are girls is so common as to go almost unnoticed, and when they are subjected to torture or ill-treatment it almost always includes abuse of a sexual nature. Many cases of sexual torture and abuse go unreported and unpunished, because the girls are too ashamed to tell anyone what has happened to them. Girls who engage in political dissent may be subject to acts of torture or ill-treatment because they are perceived as particularly dangerous in having stepped outside their accepted social role. Girls who have not been politically active may still be tortured for information about the activities of male family members, or in reprisal for the action of fathers or brothers. In armed conflict, the rape of women and girls has long been seen as a particularly effective tactic for terrorizing and taunting the enemy.

Abuses by private individuals

The challenge for human rights work may be to revise the framework in which human rights groups have traditionally looked at torture: the most dangerous place for children can be their home, where they should be safest. They are more likely to be beaten, sexually abused, abducted or subjected to harmful traditional practices or mental violence by family members than anyone else.[20] Those in "surrogate" homes, such as care institutions, who are regularly beaten up or raped, or child prostitutes who are repeatedly subjected to sexual violence, are as much at risk as children in police custody. Domestic abuse, although outside the scope of the present study, is an area that must be explored if we are to understand and work against the full range of violence against children.[21]

Corporal punishment

Corporal punishment is another complex area, both in terms of law and in its application to children.[22] The legislation of many countries allows for the corporal punishment of children in both schools and the family, mostly based on the idea that "reasonable chastisement" of children is permissible. In many countries, in fact, the physical punishment of children is the only form of interpersonal violence sanctioned by the law, although even trivial assaults on adults are usually criminalized.

Judicial corporal punishments are a form of torture or other cruel, inhuman or degrading punishment and are thus banned under international law. AI is categorically opposed to the corporal punishment — either judicial or disciplinary — of both juvenile and adult prisoners. Corporal punishment is specifically prohibited for juveniles by the Beijing Rules[23] and the UN Rules for the Protection of Juveniles Deprived of their Liberty,[24] and less explicitly by the Children's Convention and the Riyadh Guidelines. In a resolution adopted in April 2000, the UN Commission on Human Rights stated that "corporal punishment, including of children, can amount to cruel, inhuman or degrading punishment or even to torture".[25] In some countries, notably Nigeria, Saudi Arabia and Singapore, children convicted of certain offences can be flogged or caned. However, the main venue for the corporal punishment of children, outside the family, is in schools.

The Special Rapporteur on torture has said that the use of corporal punishment is inconsistent with the prohibition of torture and other cruel, inhuman or degrading treatment or punishment. In his recent report on Kenya, he called for the repeal of corporal punishment in schools, and for the "diligent prosecution" of school personnel for assault or battery in cases in which pupils had suffered injuries ranging from "cuts and bruises to psychological damage and severe injuries, such as broken bones, internal bleeding, knocked-out teeth..."[26]

Although corporal punishment in schools may not always constitute a form of torture or cruel, inhuman or degrading treatment,[27] the UN Committee on the Rights of the Child states unambiguously that corporal punishment in schools is "incompatible" with the Children's Convention, and regularly urges states to prohibit corporal punishment not just in schools and other institutions, but also "in the family and in society at large."[28] Although the Children's Convention does not explicitly prohibit corporal punishment, it does enjoin states parties to protect children from "all forms of physical or mental violence", and to "ensure that school discipline is administered in a manner consistent with the child's human dignity and in conformity with the present Convention."[29]

The Committee recommends that the ban on corporal punishment should extend to the family. Many states allow corporal punishment or "reasonable chastisement" within the family, a practice the Committee has condemned: "As for corporal punishment, few countries have clear laws on this question. Certain states have tried to distinguish between the correction of children and excessive violence. In reality, the dividing line between the two is artificial. It is very easy to pass from one stage to the other. It is also a question of principle. If it is not permissible to beat an adult, why should it be permissible to do so to a child?"[30] AI has called for the abolition of corporal punishment in schools.

Effects of torture on children

© AI

Drawing by a former child soldier from Uganda, where thousands of children have been abducted and forced to work for the Lord's Resistance Army.

Other special considerations that mark out a difference between adults and children concern the threshold of pain and suffering. It is commonly held that the special vulnerability of children renders them more susceptible to the physical and psychological effects of torture.[31] Younger children, in particular, have a lower threshold of pain; and physical or mental abuse may have a much more profound impact on the body and mind of a developing child than on an adult. Treatment like prolonged solitary confinement, for instance, may be held to be ill-treatment in the case of an adult, but for a young child the experience may be so terrifying as to amount to torture. The Special Rapporteur on torture has said that inadequate conditions of detention could constitute torture for some children because of their "special vulnerability". The age of the child is similarly important; a five-year-old will probably be more terrified by a beating than a 17-year-old. Conversely a very young child may find certain experiences — being taken hostage with his or her mother, for instance — less frightening than a child old enough to understand the motives behind the perpetrators' actions. Gender is also a factor: girls in custody may suffer more if they have a well-founded fear of rape or sexual abuse, whether or not such abuse takes place.

While it may be true that children recover more quickly than adults from superficial injuries, more serious trauma may disrupt or distort normal growth patterns or cause permanent weakness or disability, particularly if proper medical attention is not made available. Beyond the physical pain, the psychological and long-term effects of torture or other violence on children are notoriously difficult to measure; the symptoms displayed by children with post-traumatic stress disorder (PTSD) show wider variation than those of adults. A detailed analysis is beyond the scope of this report, although some general observations can be made about the kinds of after-effects tortured children are likely to suffer. These observations are based largely on work with children who have been tortured or ill-treated in conflict situations, or because of the political affiliations of their family.33

The amount and effect of the trauma suffered is necessarily related to the age and maturity of the child as well as the kind of torture or ill-treatment they have been subjected to, and is mediated by other factors, including the child's own personality and the strength of family and community support. There are a range of symptoms, which affect most child victims of PTSD to some degree; these include sleep disturbances, nightmares, difficulty in concentration, and fears of death or injury. The

© Panos/Betty Press

Children at this Unaccompanied Children's Centre in Rwanda undergo role-play therapy to help them overcome the trauma of conflict.

severity and extent of the torture or ill-treatment suffered is key to determining the long-term consequences; long-lasting or repeated exposure to torture or ill-treatment is more likely to result in permanent personality changes.

The age and maturity of the child are important factors to consider separately; the physical and emotional reactions of a four-year-old are going to be very different from those of an older adolescent. The developmental achievements specific to each age group in the area of cognition, emotions and social relationships will all influence a child's reaction to torture and ill-treatment. Although individual responses will always vary, there is an identified set of "typical reactions" for each stage of childhood.[34]

Effects of torture on young children

Very young children often become highly fearful following a stressful experience and react strongly to all things that remind them of it. Their speech and behavioural patterns may regress. Because their view of the world is largely self-referential, they tend to believe that everything that happens must somehow relate to them; if they or their family members have been tortured, they often believe that it must be because they themselves are "bad" or responsible in some way. This can lead to feelings of overwhelming guilt or depression, which the young child cannot articulate and resolve.[35] Children aged between about six and 12 are old enough to understand the meaning of the stressful experiences they have suffered, and to recall events in a logical way. They often react to trauma through re-enacting the incident and fantasizing about different outcomes, particularly ones in which they prevented the tragedy from happening. They may imagine that they warned their family and neighbours that soldiers were about to raid the village, and everyone escaped, or that their father was not at home when the police came to take him away. If they themselves have been hurt, they tend to become obsessively fearful and withdrawn. Children in this age group accept the finality of death, and do not keep expecting the dead person to return, so may grieve more for lost parents than their younger brothers and sisters would do.[36] They quickly adopt the ethos of their social situation, so that children living through a war may internalize ideas that killing is the normal way to resolve conflict. Children of all ages who have been the victims or witnesses of torture or arbitrary brutality often find it difficult to develop trust in others, which can affect their ability to form close social relationships.[37]

Effects of torture on adolescents

Adolescents, who make up the largest percentage of child victims of torture or ill-treatment, have a more complex range of responses, and may be as vulnerable as younger children to stressful experiences. Most are already undergoing profound emotional and physical changes, and may be separated from, or in the process of separating from, their families. Many are expected to function like adults, and have the cognitive ability to understand what has happened to them or their community, but still do not have the emotional maturity to cope with it. Teenagers who suffer torture in conflict situations, many of whom also see their community and whole way of life destroyed, may feel they did not do enough to protect themselves, their family or their friends, and may then be overcome by hopelessness, guilt and depression.[38] One of the aims of torture is often to make the victim feel helpless and disempowered; there can be few easier targets than an adolescent with a tenuous grip on his or her own self-confidence.

The role of the family

Children are uniquely dependent, both physically and emotionally, on their parents or other adult carers, and are thus extremely susceptible to vicarious torture or ill-treatment. The effect on a child of watching their mother or father arrested, tortured or killed, or of having a parent or sibling "disappear" without trace, can be a form of psychological torture that may last a lifetime.[39]

The role of the family is crucial in determining the extent of the damage sustained. Children who have been tortured or ill-treated may suffer much harsher effects if they have also seen their parents subjected to similar treatment; both because the parent has failed to protect them and because it is a further confirmation that the world as they knew it has suddenly turned upside down. Moreover, parents who are themselves recovering from severe abuse may not have the emotional resources needed to recognize or help alleviate the symptoms of trauma or distress in their children.[40] Jacobo Timerman, in his famous recollection of the Argentinian "Dirty War", said: "Of all the dramatic situations I witnessed in clandestine prisons, nothing can compare to those family groups who were tortured often together, sometimes separately but in view of one another, or in different cells while one was aware of the other being tortured. Their entire affective world... collapses with a kick in the father's genitals, a smack on the mother's face, an obscene insult to the sister, or the sexual violation of a daughter. Suddenly an entire culture based on familial love, devotion, the capacity for mutual sacrifice collapses."[41]

Cultural norms

Cultural norms also shape a child's perception of what constitutes torture or ill-treatment. Children who grow up in a milieu in which violence is commonplace may be better equipped to deal with physical abuse than adults who have never been confronted by it. However, the same children who can deal with a smack or a blow with what appears to be equanimity may never have been alone in their lives, and may find isolation — even being locked up by themselves in a cell overnight — almost impossible to bear. What constitutes degrading treatment is particularly culturally specific. A girl from a conservative tradition may find even partial exposure of her body humiliating; some children may feel punishments that are demeaning, or that destroy their dignity, are worse than physical pain.

Political activism

Some children have the active support of a community beyond their immediate family. In many countries, children who are political activists know that they risk a serious beating or worse if they fall into the hands of the security forces. They may have discussed and mentally prepared themselves for the possibility of being tortured should they be detained or captured. Children who are tortured for their own activism, such as the Palestinian boys who were active in stone throwing and street demonstrations during *the intifada*, sometimes receive a great deal of community support and acclaim as a result. In some cases this can help them transform the experience into a source of pride, which can help overcome the pain.[42]

Pamela Reynolds, a South African activist, has written of the most repressive years of the anti-apartheid struggle: "There was widespread suffering among the young yet among those formally committed to political activism there was a widespread subscription to a particular stance with regard to pain. It was held that one suffered for the cause; that pain and suffering were to be anticipated along with political engagement; that those who had undergone any form of political induction would prepare to handle extreme pain; that it was assumed that others suffered more than oneself; and that pain was not a topic for discussion except where actual attention, physical or psychological, was required."[43] While not underplaying the trauma that many of the children suffered, she emphasizes that we should not underestimate the motivation and commitment of political activists and the support they can draw upon, or the power of local healing processes.

Psychological recovery from a traumatic event may be easier for those who are able to attach meaning to the incident, and understand it in the context of their sense of self and surroundings.[44] The physical pain and suffering may be the same, but a child who has been tortured because of a political or religious belief may at least have a basis for understanding what has happened to them. A child who is tortured at random, or in place of someone else, is not likely to find any similar way of normalizing the experience. The key difference is that those who are tortured because of something they have chosen — a political or religious commitment, for instance — are able to feel that they were tortured for their support of a just cause, and are less likely to be haunted by the guilt so many torture victims feel.

Social exclusion

Children who live and work in the streets may also understand that they are in danger if they fall into the hands of local police or security agents, but are missing the support and affirmation of strong community and family networks. Getting picked up by the police and savagely beaten may confirm their fear of being outsiders who do not belong to society and cannot be expected to conform to its expectations. In the wake of such an attack, a spiral in which greater alienation leads to further anti-social behaviour may be initiated or accelerated.

Mental illness or disability

A substantial proportion of children in detention suffer forms of mental illness or disability, ranging from retardation to psychotic disorders, which often go undiagnosed or untreated.[45] Some have ended up in detention because of behaviour resulting directly or indirectly from their mental illness, some have become mentally ill as a result of abusive conditions of incarceration. In many cases, the condition is exacerbated by substance abuse or addiction. These children are doubly vulnerable, and so should benefit from protections designed to address their high-risk situation and more specialized needs.[46] Although such protections may exist in law, they are seldom available in practice. Under international standards, all children in detention are entitled to medical treatment,[47] but even basic medical care is lacking in many juvenile detention facilities, and mental health provisions are frequently non-existent. When treatment is inadequate or unavailable, mentally-ill juveniles tend to suffer an intensification of their disability, which of itself may amount to cruel, inhuman or degrading treatment. When the mentally ill are subjected to ill-treatment such as solitary confinement, confinement in a dark or soundless room, or incommunicado detention, the effects of such ill-treatment may be exacerbated, causing their condition to degenerate further. Children who suffer from mental illness may not be fully capable of forming or expressing opinions about their own treatment, or may express views harmful to their own well-being. The standard of "best interests of the child" in such cases must be carefully balanced against the child's evolving right to make their own decisions, and their right to be involved in all decisions affecting their own welfare.

A hidden phenomenon?

It is sometimes said that the torture of children is "invisible". This can be at least partly attributed to a general disbelief that torture could be perpetrated against children. We also tend to think of torture as an atrocity inflicted by an agent of the state on a political prisoner in an underground cell. Children are less likely than adults to be tortured because of their own political beliefs (although they may be tortured because of the political beliefs of their parents); the torture of children is seldom a response to an overt political challenge. But it is also the case that children are more vulnerable to abuse at home, by their parents or family, than at the hands of state actors. Domestic violence, by its nature, is almost always "hidden", and so difficult to investigate and punish.

Yet even the torture of children by state agents and their henchmen is likely to be significantly under-reported. AI and other human rights organizations have documented a substantial number of cases concerning children. But those cases that have come to light are probably no more than the tip of a large iceberg. Children rarely have adequate means of protecting themselves or seeking redress. They are unlikely to be confident or articulate enough to maintain their allegations against adults and against the powers of the adult world. Many victims remain quiet because they have been threatened with further violence to themselves or their families if they tell anyone what has happened. In cases where children in detention make allegations of ill-treatment, or complain about foul conditions, they may not be taken seriously. Moreover, they are usually forced to direct their complaints to their warders, who may be the very people responsible for the abuse. Assumptions about the unreliability of children as witnesses frequently lead to their complaints or requests for help being disbelieved or ignored. Children may not know their rights, and even if they do know them, are less likely to have access to a lawyer or to be in contact with someone willing to make the matter public, much less take it to the national or international level.

The most common form of state torture against children is probably the beating of young criminal suspects in police custody. Although the situation of juveniles in custody is monitored closely by a number of local and national NGOs, particularly in Latin America, there has been little popular or international mobilization on behalf of children detained for criminal offences. In some countries, violence against such children may be seen as "juvenile delinquents getting what they deserve", and there is often popular support for "social cleansing" operations in which law enforcement officials use violence and intimidation to clear the streets of children regarded as potential offenders.

Juvenile criminal suspects will almost invariably be from the poorest or marginalized sectors of society, and discrimination against such groups often contributes to the lack of action against their torture or ill-treatment. For all of these reasons, the torture of children in the context of criminal investigations is certainly going to be under-reported.

The systematic under-reporting of abuses against children may also occur because many such incidents are regarded as private matters, rather than human rights issues. The physical

The beating of children or adults detained for criminal offences is in some countries so common that even the victims themselves do not regard it as torture or ill-treatment, but as a normal consequence of arrest. The pragmatic responses of children in South Africa, who participated in a series of workshops on a proposed Child Justice Bill, suggest that they take the possibility of ill-treatment in detention for granted. When asked how police procedures for dealing with children in custody could be improved, their two suggestions were that detained children should have prompt access to medical attention in order to ensure that evidence of any injury sustained during arrest could be formally noted, and second, that policemen should be punished should an assault occur. It apparently did not occur to them to suggest that the police should be prevented from beating children in custody in the first place.[48]

abuse of children in the workplace, which may sometimes amount to torture or ill-treatment, is often thought of as the responsibility of the parent or guardian to resolve, rather than an obligation of the state. Corporal punishment of children in schools is still widely accepted, and sometimes defended as an aid to learning, even though the punishments themselves may amount to ill-treatment or torture. Other forms of abuse which could be conducive to torture, such as bonded labour, trafficking, or work in hazardous conditions, are usually described as social issues, rather than human rights problems.

Impunity

Children are tortured because they are caught up in wars or other conflicts, for political activism or alleged criminality, or because they are socially marginal. Children are sometimes targeted simply because of the fact that they are children, and are tortured as surrogates, to punish parents or other family members, or to force family members to confess or turn themselves in. More often, however, children are tortured for the same reasons as adults: they are accused of breaking the law, they are on the "wrong side" in a conflict, or they belong to an ethnic or religious group likely to suffer discrimination.

One of the strands that unites these disparate groups of children is the almost complete impunity enjoyed by those who torture or ill-treat them. Where allegations of torture have been made, one factor common to most cases is the lack of any proper investigation. Allegations of torture against police officers are often investigated by the suspect's colleagues or even accomplices. When flawed investigations fail to lead to prosecutions, it is possible for the authorities at the highest level to deny the existence of torture, and to evade taking any proper action to prevent it. States have an obligation to carry out "a prompt and impartial investigation wherever there is reasonable ground to believe that an act of torture has been committed", and to ensure that the victim is protected from intimidation or ill-treatment as a consequence of making a complaint.[49] AI's research shows that those who torture children are seldom brought to justice and only then if the case generates substantial public or international outrage. When torturers are not brought to justice, it lets others know they can commit the same crimes with impunity, and the cycle of violence continues.[50]

The cases that follow in the next chapters are thus unusual only in that they are documented; most children suffer in silence, their stories never told, their tormentors never called to account. Many of these cases are not easy to read. Children who are survivors of torture have often given testimonies to AI investigators, and as far as possible, we have tried to use their own words, to let them tell their own stories. These cases are drawn from all over the world, and were chosen because they are representative of the many situations and contexts in which children can be abused. The fact that a country does not appear in this report does not mean that it does not torture its children; and countries listed here do not include all of those where torture is most widely practised. We see the same patterns of abuse around the world: the ill-treatment of children in police custody in China mirrors the ill-treatment of children in custody in Brazil; there is little difference between conditions of detention in Paraguay and in Russia; and violence against children by armies and armed opposition groups takes equally devastating forms in countries as far apart as Sierra Leone and Afghanistan. No region of the world can be said to treat its children better than any other.

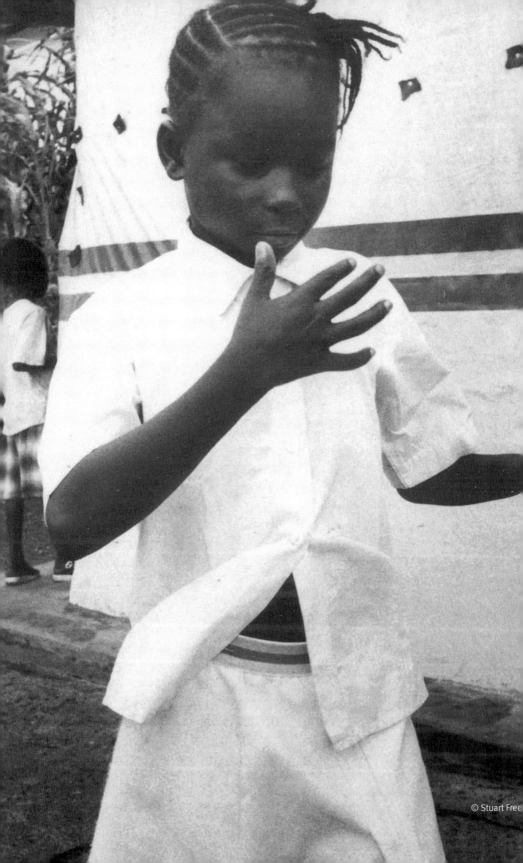

2: TORTURE OF CHILDREN DURING CONFLICT

Armed conflict

War is a daily reality for millions of children. Some have never known any other life – they have grown up in the midst of civil wars, guerrilla insurgency, or long-term occupation by a foreign army. For others, the world is suddenly turned upside down when invasion or forced internal displacement drives them onto the road as refugees or displaced persons, often separated from their families. Today's conflicts are largely fought inside states, rather than between them, putting children's homes, schools and communities in the firing line. Children can be the direct targets of torture or ill-treatment in such conflicts, in which the objectives are less the acquisition of territory than the subjugation or extermination of a specific group of people. These internal conflicts are often linked to the disintegration of state structures, which can create situations of such anarchy that almost all the mechanisms in place to protect children's rights no longer function.

Children injured in armed conflicts are often innocent bystanders, but some are targeted deliberately by security forces and armed opposition groups, in retribution or to provoke outrage in each other's communities. Some, mainly girls, are singled out for sexual abuse. Young men are often picked up without charge, on the assumption that they participate in, or sympathize with, armed opposition groups. Many children are killed or tortured simply because they live in an "enemy zone", or because of the politics, religion or ethnic origin of their family.

In Afghanistan, more than two decades of civil war have had a brutal impact on whole generations of the country's children. Thousands have been subjected to deliberate and arbitrary killings and torture at the hands of the numerous armed political groups. Many more have been killed or mutilated by the millions of landmines littering the country. Hundreds of thousands have been

A young girl whose hand was amputated by rebel forces in Freetown, Sierra Leone, in January 1999.

27

Even in the midst of war the international prohibition of torture still applies. International humanitarian law, also known as the laws of war, provides general protection for all civilians, including civilian children, and special protection to children as persons who are particularly vulnerable. Children taking part in the hostilities are also protected. The four Geneva Conventions of 1949 and their two Additional Protocols of 1977 are the main treaties which codify the laws of war. Under the Geneva Conventions, torture in an international armed conflict is a "grave breach" of the laws of war — a war crime. The principle of special protection for children is explicitly laid down in Article 77 of Protocol I, relating to international armed conflicts, which says that "children shall be the object of special respect and shall be protected against any form of indecent assault." Article 4 of Protocol II, which applies to internal conflicts, similarly requires special measures for the protection of children. Both Protocols also include provisions on the protection of children engaged in the conflict, requiring, for instance, that captured combatants under the age of 15 should still receive the special protections afforded to civilian children, and fixing the minimum age limit for the execution of the death penalty at 18 years. Torture and ill-treatment are also prohibited under Article 3 common to all four Geneva Conventions, which applies both to governments and armed opposition groups in internal armed conflicts. Torture in violation of common Article 3 is recognized as a war crime under the Rome Statute of the International Criminal Court, which was adopted in 1998 but had not yet come into force by October 2000.

killed or maimed in indiscriminate bombing and shelling of their homes, schools or playing fields.

Girls in Afghanistan have been abducted by local warring commanders, either for their own sexual purposes or to be sold into prostitution. Girls — and some boys — have been raped or sexually assaulted. In March 1994, a 15-year-old girl was repeatedly raped in her house in Kabul's Chel Sotoon district after armed guards entered the house and killed her father for allowing her to go to school: "They shot my father right in front of me. He was a shop-keeper. It was nine o'clock at night. They came to our house and told him they had orders to kill him because he allowed me to go to school. The *Mujahideen* had already stopped me from going to school, but that was not enough. They then came and killed my father. I cannot describe what they did to me after killing my father..."

There have been reports of the *Taleban* carrying out wide-scale massacres and acts of torture. Children were among some 70 civilians who were killed by armed *Taleban* guards in September 1997 in Qezelabad village near Mazar-e Sharif. Survivors said that an eight-year-old child had been decapitated, and two boys of about 12 were held by the guards and had their arms and hands broken with stones. As the *Taleban* have clamped down on political activists who peacefully oppose the continuing war, hundreds of children have been held hostage in place of their fathers who have escaped arrest. Among them were nine boys who were taken hostage in Kabul and other parts of the country in 1998. These children spent several months in detention, where they were reportedly subjected to torture and ill-treatment.

The trauma of experiencing such brutality and being surrounded by violence, fear and hardship has deeply affected the children of Afghanistan. In 1997 UNICEF released a large-scale study on the effects of the conflict on children. Some 72 per cent of the children interviewed had experienced the death of a relative. Nearly all of the children interviewed had witnessed acts of violence. Two thirds of them had seen dead bodies or body parts and nearly half had seen people killed during rocket and artillery attacks. A disturbing 90 per cent believed they would die during the conflict.

The torture of children in Sierra Leone is among the most egregious examples of violence and terror against children that AI has ever documented. Throughout the nine years of civil war, children have suffered disproportionately and on an unprecedented scale. Thousands have been killed or subjected to mutilation, rape, and abduction during systematic campaigns of atrocities committed largely by forces of the Revolutionary United Front (RUF) and the Armed Forces Revolutionary Council (AFRC). Almost all of the thousands of girls and women who have been abducted by armed political groups have been raped and forced into sexual slavery.[51] In January 1999, following the attack on the capital Freetown by RUF and AFRC forces, some 4,000 children were abducted, most of them girls, and several thousand people, including children, were killed or mutilated. Thousands of children, both boys and girls, have been abducted and forced to fight and hundreds of thousands of others have become refugees or internally displaced, often separated from their families.

One of the most cruel and inhumane aspects of the conflict has been the tactic of cutting off the arms, hands or feet of civilians, including children and even babies. An eight-year-old girl, whose right hand was amputated in Northern Province in 1998, told AI representatives in May 2000: "The rebels came to Kabala. When they came to our house they forced us to go outside. They said that they were going to kill all of us and one of them ordered another rebel to go and get a machete. They pushed me to the ground and then cut off my hand. They called my mother and they cut her hand off too. Nine other people had their hands cut off. The rebels told us to go to President Tejan Kabbah and ask for new hands. The others were all killed. I don't know how many ... I am now living here in this camp with my mother and I am going to school. My arm still hurts."

A peace agreement between the government and the RUF was signed in July 1999, and initially reduced the scale of abuses. The agreement provided a blanket amnesty for crimes committed between 1991, when the conflict began, and July 1999 — including the rape of tens of thousands of girls and women, the deliberate mutilation of thousands of men, women and children, and countless other gross abuses of human rights. Yet the pattern of rape, mutilations and killings committed with total impunity re-emerged after only a few months.

The political and security situation deteriorated still further in early May 2000, when some 500 UN peace-keepers were captured by rebel forces. The resumption of hostilities resulted in an increase in abuses against civilians, including children. In August 2000 the UN Security Council passed a resolution to establish an independent special court for Sierra Leone to try those accused of crimes against humanity, war crimes and other serious violations of international law, as well as crimes under Sierra Leone law.

Refugees and internally displaced children

Armed conflict has forced millions of children around the world to flee their homes in search of refuge. Sometimes they go with their families, sometimes alone; many get separated on the way. In Africa alone, conflict has forced more than 20 million people from their homes. About five million are refugees who have found asylum in a neighbouring country; many more — an estimated 16 million — are internally displaced persons (IDPs) within their own country. Refugees and IDPs are at the mercy of whoever controls the territory they are in, and are extremely vulnerable to abuse. In Sudan, where a long-running civil war involves governmental armed forces, pro-government militias and armed opposition groups, 4.5 million people are internally displaced and the state has disintegrated into patches of territory controlled by competing armed factions. "N.J.", an 11-year-old girl, lives with her family in an IDP camp on the outskirts of Khartoum, the capital of Sudan. In May 1999 she was picked up by police officers, who mistook her for a vagrant child, and taken to Soba police station in Khartoum, where a policeman undressed her by force, threatening to beat her if she resisted. He then raped her in the presence of three other policemen. She was later taken to hospital, where doctors found medical evidence consistent with her account.

Four policemen have been charged — one accused of rape and the others of complicity. However, the police officers investigating the case have delayed the trial by insisting that N.J. be subjected to a further medical examination to confirm the rape. An invasive medical examination so long after the event would not provide any additional evidence, and would be a source of considerable emotional pain for the girl, who is said to be already extremely traumatized. N.J. and her lawyers were reportedly harassed by the police in mid-2000, and the investigation into her case appears to be stalled.

In the Russian Federation, more than 200,000 Chechens have fled into the neighbouring Republic of Ingushetia. Many more IDPs are trapped inside Chechnya. Since September 1999, when a renewed Russian military offensive was launched against

© Reuters/Popperfoto

Chechen refugees at a makeshift kitchen in Karabulak Camp, Ingushetia, July 2000.

Chechnya, civilians have been fleeing the conflict areas.

Russian forces have been detaining people at checkpoints and in the territories under their control; often while carrying out identity checks on civilian convoys fleeing to Ingushetia. Witnesses say that children as young as 10 have been detained on suspicion of belonging to armed Chechen groups. The detainees are sent to "filtration" centres where they are held without access to their relatives, lawyers or the outside world. The testimonies of the survivors confirm that the men, women and children held in these camps are routinely and systematically tortured: they are variously beaten with hammers and clubs, tortured with electric shocks and tear gas, and raped.

Former detainees of Chernokozovo "filtration" centre told AI that in January 2000 they saw a 14-year-old girl being raped by several prison guards in the corridor outside their cells. The girl was visiting her detained mother and, for the price of 5,000 rubles, had been told she would be permitted a five-minute meeting. Her short meeting became a four-day ordeal during which she was locked in a cell, beaten and repeatedly raped by guards.

"Musa",[52] who was held in Chernokozovo "filtration" centre between 16 January and 5 February 2000, was severely beaten and tortured several times each day during his detention, and has been left with a fractured spine, which may cause permanent paralysis. He said that a 16-year-old boy called Albert was brought to his cell after being raped with batons and severely beaten by prison guards. One of his ears had been cut off and the guards referred to him by the female name of "Maria". Musa said that at one point during his 21-day detention, he shared a cell with a 17-year-old boy, whose teeth had been sawn off with a metal file and whose lips were shredded, leaving him unable to eat, drink or speak. Musa estimated that 10 to 15 new detainees were brought to the centre each day. Among those he saw were 13- and 14-year-old girls.

In March 2000, witnesses told AI that a 14-year-old girl, originally from Urus-Martan, had died in detention in Chernokozovo at the beginning of the year — allegedly as a result of being tortured and ill-treated, including being repeatedly raped by the guards.

Torture as a weapon of war

Armies and paramilitary groups may use torture and ill-treatment as a tactic to terrorize and subjugate the civilian population, particularly in areas where support for opposition forces may be high. Children are particularly vulnerable in such cases; they are often singled out because they represent the real and psychological future of a community. The rape and sexual abuse of women and children by police and security forces in areas of armed conflict in India has been a common means of abusing and terrorizing the civilian population. Although the authorities have taken action against the perpetrators in a few cases, the climate of impunity and the difficulties faced by victims in seeking redress contribute to the continuation of these abuses.

On 23 May 1997, soldiers from the 16 Rajput regiment in the state of Assam in India conducted a raid on a village in the Kamrup district of Assam, in order to round up suspected members of armed opposition groups. While they searched the houses, the villagers were forced to assemble in a field. Several soldiers reportedly raped Santhali Bodo, aged 17, and Rangeela Basumatari, aged 15, in front of their assembled neighbours. On the following day, soldiers from the same regiment reportedly came again to the village, went to the house of Dayaram Rava and raped his daughters Runumi Basumatari, aged 16, and Thingigi Basumatari, aged 17. The military had cordoned off the area, and villagers were forbidden to move freely around, so the incidents could not be reported to the police for several days, and the girls were unable to get to a doctor for medical examinations. When a complaint could finally be lodged at the Tamulpur police station, it appears to have been ignored. AI has pursued the apparent lack of any investigation with the Indian government, but has received no response.

In Manipur in July 1998, five young boys were on their way home from fishing in the river near Andro village in Thoubal district. They were stopped by a soldier from the Andro army camp, who had already halted three boys herding cattle. The soldier, from the 17 Rajput Rifles regiment, ordered all of the boys to stand off at a distance, with their heads between their legs except seven-year-old Boboy, nine-year-old Joychandra, and 10-year-old Joykumar. These three boys were ordered to stand out of sight behind bushes, and were forced to perform fellatio on the soldier for about half an hour. The soldier then beat up the elder boys, three of whom are Joychandra's brothers. A complaint was filed at the local police station, accompanied by a widespread public campaign by local women and youth organizations for an inquiry. An army investigation into the incident was opened, but at the same time many of those involved in the case were pressured to withdraw their complaint. A military court of inquiry in August 1998 discounted the allegations of sexual abuse, and a government press release noted that the soldier had only "lightly hit once each with a twig" three of the older boys. Videotapes of Boboy, Joychandra and Joykumar describing the incident were viewed by an independent psychiatric expert in the UK, who found their testimony to be "indicative of abuse".

Young people, particularly boys, are sometimes picked up without charge, on the suspicion that they participate in or sympathize with armed groups. In Algeria, thousands of detainees, including children, have reportedly complained of torture and ill-treatment since 1992, but AI does not know of any cases in which allegations of torture have been thoroughly investigated, preventative measures taken and members of the security forces brought to justice for torturing detainees. Hassan Cherif and his brother Hakim, aged 17 and 18 respectively, were reportedly arrested on 2 August 1996 and kept for 17 days in incommunicado detention at the commissariat of Bab Ezzouar, Algiers, on suspicion of having links with an armed group. Both are said to have been subjected to electric shocks and the *chiffon* — a common method of torture in Algeria — in which large quantities of dirty water mixed with chemicals are poured down the detainee's throat and a cloth is stuffed into his mouth, resulting in near-suffocation and severe swelling of the stomach. Hassan was also hit across the face with a gun so hard it broke his nose; his brother Hakim is said to have sustained a broken leg. According to their account, they were also threatened with rape.[53] A request for a medical examination by their lawyer on 15 September 1996 had reportedly not been responded to by April 1997, although the government claims that a medical examination carried out in October 1996 concluded that no torture had taken place.[54] No copy of the medical report has been made available to AI.

In Sri Lanka, torture by both sides has been reported in the context of the ongoing armed conflict between the security forces and the Liberation Tigers of Tamil Eelam (LTTE), fighting for an independent state, Eelam, in the north and east of the country. There have been several chilling reports of the torture of Tamil children taken into custody in order to force a member of their family to hand him or herself over, or on suspicion of being members of the LTTE.

Vallipuram Suganthi, a 15-year-old Tamil girl, was reportedly arrested on 10 July 1997 by 12 police officers and taken to Wellawatte police station, where she was severely beaten and threatened with rape if she did not sign a statement about her involvement with the LTTE, which she eventually did. She was later transferred to the Crime Detection Bureau, where her captors allegedly beat her over the head with a wooden stick and threatened to kill her. She was eventually released, and underwent medical treatment at the Family Rehabilitation Centre of Colombo.[55]

Sinnarasa Anthonymala, a girl from Jaffna, was arrested by the navy in July 1995 when she was 15 years old. After she was released in January 1999, she told AI how she was held naked and taken for interrogation by the navy up to three times a day throughout her stay at the Kankesanthurai navy camp. She was hung upside down and beaten on her legs, burned with cigarettes, given electric shocks and burned with heated metal rods. Over a month later, she was transferred to the custody of the police in Colombo, where she was cut in the back of the neck, hit in the mouth and on the legs with a piece of wood, and forced to sign seven statements. In October 1997, a Judicial Medical Officer (JMO) in Colombo examined Sinnarasa Anthonymala and found evidence of at least 46 wounds on her body; in his report to the High Court the JMO said that her scars were consistent with injuries sustained in 1995. Four months after she was released, Anthonymala was rearrested in April 1999 under another charge ("illegal presence in a prohibited zone"). She is currently held at Welikade women's prison. The trial is pending.

Children are sometimes targeted simply because of the fact that they are young — their vulnerability turned to good advantage by their attackers. They may be tortured as surrogates, to punish parents or other family members who are not in custody, or to force family members to confess or to give themselves or their comrades up. According to the UN Special Rapporteur on torture, seven-month-old Muhammad Ardiansyah was reportedly suspended by his legs and left hanging in the sun for several hours in Aceh, Indonesia, in February 1998. The Indonesian security forces reportedly wanted his mother to reveal the whereabouts of her husband, suspected of separatist activity.[56] Both mother and child were later released.

In some cases, the perpetrators are paramilitary forces linked to government soldiers. In Colombia, 17-year-old Elena Morales Souto was dragged from her home on 20 July 1997 by a group of heavily armed men, who allegedly identified themselves as paramilitaries from Abrego and Ocaña. A short distance from her house, she was beaten and threatened with having her throat cut if she did not disclose the whereabouts of her husband, Hugo Umaña, and her father, Luis Morales Perez. The girl allegedly recognized one of her aggressors at the military barracks of the Santander Battalion on 23 July. Other members of her family, including nine children, were allegedly tortured physically and psychologically at their home by paramilitaries. Before withdrawing, the paramilitaries told the family that they would come back and kill them all, down to the smallest child, if they ever found Luis Morales Perez or Hugo Umaña there.[57]

Children may also be tortured or ill-treated as a threat or punishment to their parents, who may be political activists or community leaders. In Guatemala, a public official reportedly raped the 12-year-old daughter of Nicolas Pichol Calel, who works on behalf of a local human rights NGO. According to accusations lodged by her family, the official raped Ana Maria Pichol Guarcas on two separate occasions in December 1999. He told Ana Maria that he would kill her and her family if she resisted further rape or reported him to the authorities. The accused, an ex-military commissioner, is the assistant mayor for a community in the municipality of San Pedro Yepocapa, Chimaltenango. Despite the death threats, Nicolas Pichol Calel lodged an accusation against the official with the Office of the Public Prosecutor, which is now in charge of the case. The official was arrested on 28 April 2000 but released four days later. Nicolas Pichol Calel said the official has repeatedly threatened him. The rape of Ana Maria and the death threats against Nicolas Pichol Calel appear to be related to his work for the *Coordinadora Nacional de Viudas de Guatemala* (CONAVIGUA), the National Coordinator of Guatemala's Widows. CONAVIGUA investigates massacres that took place during the army's brutal counter-insurgency campaign of the late 1970s and early 1980s, in order to bring the perpetrators to justice and to secure compensation for the victims' families. Members of the organization, and their families, have been subjected to constant intimidation by the local authorities. This intimidation has escalated since Nicolas Pichol Calel lodged the rape accusation.

In Saudi Arabia, an 11-year-old boy was arrested in May 1999 and beaten by the *Mutawa'een* (religious police) who were seeking to arrest his parents. The boy, who was a non-Saudi Arabian national, was then taken away and kept in an orphanage for two days with no knowledge of his parents' whereabouts. He told AI: "I really did not know where my parents were and was very scared because I did not know how long I was going to stay there ... I saw children being beaten by a teacher using sticks and they were crying ... [I also] saw the teacher bending children's fingers backwards and they were crying..." His parents were later arrested.

Youth activism

In countries in political turmoil, or embroiled in internal armed conflict, students and young people can be at the forefront of struggles for democracy, self-determination or social change. Governments who view political activity as a threat to state security may use torture as a means of suppressing dissent. Young activists involved in protests and demonstrations, for instance, may be arrested and tortured in an attempt to intimidate them, and to dissuade them and others from taking part in further political activity. Children and adults arrested for political offences — particularly when they are suspected of involvement in armed groups — are frequently held in incommunicado detention, which greatly increases their chances of being tortured or ill-treated.[58] Torture most often occurs during a detainee's first hours or days in custody. If a child spends these vulnerable hours in secret detention, cut off from the outside world, from the support of family and the advice of a lawyer, at the mercy of his or her captors, the effect can only be a deep sense of terror and powerlessness.

Hundreds of Palestinian children have been arrested by the

Israeli military for offences such as membership of illegal organizations and stone-throwing. They are often detained incommunicado, and held for days before being brought before a court. Some are beaten, deprived of sleep, food and drink, subjected to threats and humiliation; some have been convicted on the basis of confessions extracted under torture. In 1999 alone, Defence of Children International's Palestinian Section documented 83 cases of Palestinian children being beaten or fired upon by members of the Israeli security forces. In August 1999 the military government lowered, from 14 to 12 years, the age at which Palestinian children could be tried in military courts and imprisoned. The courts increased the tariff sentence for stone-throwing by children from four weeks' to four months' imprisonment.

Su'ad Hilmi Ghazal, a Palestinian schoolgirl from Sebastiya village, has been detained without trial since she was arrested in December 1998 at the age of 15. She had been taken into custody after a woman from Shavei Shomron settlement claimed that Su'ad had tried to stab her. At the time of her arrest, according to Su'ad, a crowd of settlers and Israeli soldiers took off her headscarf, kicked her repeatedly and beat her with rifle butts. The assault lasted some 15 minutes. She was reportedly then taken by soldiers to a military office, with her hands so tightly bound they bled, and questioned for some 10 hours, while her interrogators swore and shouted at her. She was eventually taken to Neve Tirza Prison inside Israel, where she was held incommunicado for about four weeks, much of the time in solitary confinement in a tiny cell. Her family was only allowed to visit her after repeated appeals from the Palestinian Red Crescent. As of August 2000, she was still being held at the prison, along with adult prisoners.

Her health has deteriorated in detention, and as a result of the beatings, she suffers from headaches and pain in her joints, hands and chest. She says she has not received adequate medical care for the injuries she sustained at the time of her arrest. A doctor who examined Su'ad in February 2000 issued a report stating that she was unfit to stand trial and in need of psychiatric treatment, adding that further detention would exacerbate her condition. Yet despite these recommendations, and the fear and confusion she continues to suffer due to the uncertainty about her future, she still had no fixed court date as of August 2000, and had not appeared before a judge since July 1999.

©Private

'Ali Mustafa Tubeh

'Ali Mustafa Tubeh, a schoolboy, was arrested by members of the Israeli security forces in south Lebanon in October 1997. His father, Mustafa Jawad Tubeh, had also been arrested in their home village of Arnun inside Israel's self-styled "security zone" in south Lebanon. 'Ali Tubeh was taken to Khiam Detention Centre where he was detained without charge or trial for over two years. Hundreds of Lebanese civilians, many of them women and children, were detained at Khiam for months or years without charge or trial. Conditions in Khiam, which was closed down when the Israeli army withdrew from Lebanon in May 2000, were harsh, and torture and ill-treatment common. Journalists who entered the prison after the Israeli pull-out found a whipping pole, electrodes, wire whips, hoods and manacles.59 'Ali Tubeh was held for nine months without being able to receive visits from his family outside the prison, or from the International Committee of the Red Cross. His mother, Zeinab Nasser, managed to see him three times while she was also detained in Khiam during late 1997. He told her that he had been made to sit in a container of water which was connected to an electrical supply, and that he had been beaten on the head. After his release in November 1999, he described the other torture he had received: "They threatened to kill me and to arrest my mother and sister. I was whipped on the feet as well as all over my body. As a result of pouring cold water on my body, I suffered from a severe cold and currently I have a tachycardia and problems with the large intestine. I had surgery on my foot because of the whipping and the doctors found many strings and pieces of metal caused by the mistakes from the surgery which I was subjected to in detention."

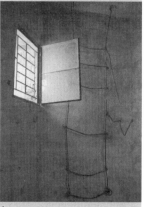

©Ina Tin/AI

Detainees were suspended from the iron bars in this interrogation room in Khiam Detention Centre. Many were beaten and subjected to electric shocks.

© Private

Phuntsog Legmon and Namdrol, in Lhasa, Tibet, wearing lay clothes, just before they staged the brief demonstration for which they were arrested and beaten.

Other children have been detained and tortured because of the peaceful expression of their political beliefs. In Tibet, a 16-year-old monk was arrested and beaten after staging a short protest with another young monk in March 1999. Phuntsog Legmon, aged 16, and 21-year-old Namdrol entered the route around Lhasa's main temple, raised their fists into the air and shouted slogans including "Free Tibet" and "Tibet is not part of China". Some reports say they were initially carrying the banned Tibetan flag. Within a few minutes, the two were detained by uniformed police, who reportedly beat them with fists and batons. In detention, according to one source, the two were severely beaten by security police: "Namdrol's mouth was so badly smashed and his broken teeth looked so horrifying that bystanders could not even look at him." In June 1999 Phuntsog Legmon was sentenced to a prison term of three years; Namdrol received a four-year sentence. The Special Rapporteur on torture has documented a number of cases in which Tibetan students have been detained and beaten for peaceful activities, including saying that Tibet was not part of China, or demanding more Tibetan teachers in their school.[60]

Child soldiers

More than 300,000 children are fighting in armed conflicts in more than 30 countries worldwide; hundreds of thousands more children have been recruited, both into governmental armed forces and armed opposition groups.[61] While most child soldiers are aged between 15 and 18, many are recruited from the age of 10 and sometimes even younger. Many child soldiers are abducted into service, or forced to join by intimidation and threats against themselves or their families; others are driven into the armed forces by poverty, alienation and discrimination.

Child soldiers aged from 12 to 17 made up at least a quarter of the Isatabu Freedom Movement fighters met by AI representatives on Guadalcanal island in the Solomon Islands. At least 100 child soldiers, some reportedly coerced into service, have been operating in the two-year ethnic conflict on the island.

Many children join armed groups because of their own experience of abuse at the hands of state authorities.

Forcible conscription by abduction is often itself an act of torture, ripping terrified children from the security of their families, often accompanied by killings, rape and severe beatings.

B., a 14-year-old girl, was abducted in Uganda in February 1997: "I had gone to the garden to collect tomatoes at around eight or nine in the morning. Suddenly, I was surrounded by about 50 rebels. They started picking tomatoes and eating them. They arrested me and started beating me terribly. Finally, I walked them to my home. We went there and collected my clothes. There, they killed my mother. They made me go, leaving behind my little brother and two little sisters. They are still very young. I was trying to explain to them that I could not leave behind the children because they were too young to fend for themselves. I was resisting. Then they started beating me until I became unconscious."

Most child soldiers get only minimal training before being thrown into the front lines of an adult war; some are used as spies, messengers, sentries, porters, servants and even sexual slaves. Casualty rates among child soldiers are generally high, because of their inexperience, fearlessness and lack of training, and because they are often used for particularly hazardous assignments, such as intelligence work or planting landmines. In recent years, there has been a trend in some countries to deliberately recruit children rather than adults. Both governments and armed groups use children because they are easier to condition into fearless killing and unthinking obedience; child soldiers are sometimes supplied with drugs and alcohol to overcome their fear or reluctance to fight. The situation is most critical in Africa and Asia, though children have been used as soldiers by governments and armed groups in the Americas, Europe and Middle East.

Child soldiers are at risk of being tortured by the enemy if caught, and by their own forces as a form of discipline or training. Children are often treated brutally and punishments for mistakes or desertion are severe; children are injured and sometimes killed during harsh training regimes. Although both boys and girls are used as fighters, girls are at particular risk of rape, sexual harassment and abuse. The severe psychological consequences of active participation in hostilities, with children both witnessing and committing atrocities, may only become apparent over a long period.

Thousands of boys and girls, some as young as five, have fought on both sides of the civil war in Sierra Leone.[62] Most of the children serving with the RUF and AFRC forces have been abducted from their homes and families and forced to fight; many were separated from their families at a very young age. Although several thousand child soldiers were released after the peace agreement was signed in July 1999, a resumption of hostilities in May 2000 resulted in the renewed recruitment of children by both opposition forces and government-allied forces.[63]

Children fighting in Sierra Leone live in constant fear. Many former child soldiers describe being threatened, intimidated and severely beaten by their own commanders. "Ibrahim",[64] now 16 and living at a centre for former child combatants, was captured by the RUF when he was about eight years old. In June 2000, Ibrahim told AI that: "Any fighter or children suspected of being reluctant to do the killings were severely beaten. We were asked to advance and to do everything possible to terrorize the civilians. During that time, one of the children asked the commander the reasons for the killings ... Sheriff Kabia, who was 17 and known as 'Crazy Jungle', was killed because he asked this question." Ibrahim also described how a 14-year-old boy was killed because he refused to cut off the hand of someone from his own village.

© CARITAS-Makeni

Several hundred schoolchildren demonstrate against the use of child soldiers, Freetown, Sierra Leone, 22 March 2000.

The psychological effects of the conflict on these children are immeasurable: many have killed, mutilated or raped and all have witnessed such atrocities. During the incursion into Freetown by the RUF and AFRC forces in January 1999 — when at least 2,000 civilians were killed, more than 500 people had limbs severed, and the rape of girls and women was systematic — it was estimated that children comprised some 10 per cent of the fighters. During the first few weeks after they are disarmed and demobilized, former child combatants are often reported to be aggressive and violent, to show other behavioural problems, to suffer nightmares, alienation, outbursts of anger and an inability to interact socially.

In northern Uganda, thousands of boys and girls have been abducted by the Lord's Resistance Army (LRA), and forced to fight the Ugandan army. The regime they endure is violent. Those caught trying to escape are killed or tortured, and both boys and girls are brutalized by being made to kill other children. Abducted children are owned by LRA commanders, with girls allocated to commanders in forced marriages and effectively held as sexual slaves. LRA commanders force children to take part in the ritualized killing of others soon after they are seized, apparently to break down resistance, destroy taboos about killing, implicate children in criminal acts and generally to terrorize them. One 15-year-old

Many are forced to kill and mutilate under the influence of drugs or alcohol. "Komba",[65] now aged 15, was captured by the RUF in 1997. He told AI in June 2000 that he was among the forces who attacked Freetown in January 1999. "My legs were cut with blades and cocaine was rubbed in the wounds. Afterwards, I felt like a big person. I saw the other people like chickens and rats. I wanted to kill them." Children who refuse to take drugs have been beaten and, in some cases, killed. "When you refuse to take drugs", one 14-year-old boy told AI, "it's called technical sabotage and you are killed."

girl who had escaped the LRA told AI that she had been forced to kill a boy who had tried to escape, and she had watched as another boy was hacked to death for not raising the alarm when a friend ran away. She herself was beaten when she dropped a water container and ran for cover under gunfire.

Those who have escaped the LRA continue to suffer. Reintegration is difficult, with children haunted psychologically and facing an immense struggle to rebuild shattered lives. The medical and social consequences are particularly bad for girls, almost all of whom are suffering from sexually transmitted diseases, and face the social stigma of rape. One 16-year-old girl said: "The Commander gave us husbands, except for the young ones, those below 13. But from 13 onwards, we

Girls in Uganda receive counselling after they were kidnapped and forced to become the "wives" of commanders in the Lord's Resistance Army in 1997.

© Magnum/Steele-Perkins

were all given as wives. There was no marriage ceremony. But if you refuse, you are killed."

The problem of child soldiers is by no means confined to Africa or to armed opposition groups. In the UK, for instance, there are more than 9,000 under-18s in the armed forces. The power and hierarchy relationships on which the armed forces are based make children especially vulnerable to ill-treatment. In August 1997, a 17-year-old girl recruit was forced to perform a sex act and was raped by a drunken instructor while she was on manoeuvres. Other incidents have included bullying, beatings and sexual abuse. The USA also allows under-18s to be recruited, and only agreed in January 2000 to ban the deployment of child soldiers in combat.

An Optional Protocol to the Children's Convention was agreed in January 2000, which establishes 18 as the minimum age for conscription and seeks to prevent the use of soldiers under the age of 18 (i.e., those who have been voluntarily recruited) in combat situations. The treaty applies to both national armed forces and to non-governmental armed groups. However, the treaty fails to establish 18 as the minimum age for voluntary recruitment into government armed forces.[66] AI and other human rights NGOs advocate the adoption of a "straight 18" policy, setting 18 as the minimum age for all forms of military recruitment and service.

Asia ranks close behind Africa in the use of tens of thousands of children as cannon-fodder. Myanmar, Sri Lanka and Afghanistan are identified as the worst affected countries in the region. Across Asia and the Pacific, children have been recruited, sometimes forcibly, into governmental armed forces, paramilitary groups or militia and armed political groups. In general, these children are required to carry out the same duties as their adult counterparts, including killing civilians and acting as porters. Most of the children suffer physical abuse and other privations within the armed forces.

In Sri Lanka, the LTTE has carried out widespread recruitment of children as combatants through propaganda, enticement or sometimes force. Although the LTTE gave commitments to the UN's Special Representative on Children and Armed Conflict, who visited Sri Lanka in May 1998, to halt

Recent developments in international law have confirmed that children under 15 should not be recruited to any armed forces (either voluntarily or by force). Any recruitment of the under-15s is a war crime under the jurisdiction of the International Criminal Court, in both international and non-international conflict. This confirms the prohibition on recruitment of child soldiers in international humanitarian law, specifically the Additional Protocols to the Geneva Conventions (Article 77(2) of Additional Protocol I, Article 4(3)(c) of Additional Protocol II).

International law unfortunately still allows the recruitment of children between 15 and 18 under certain circumstances. The Convention on the Rights of the Child (Article 38(2)) allows the recruitment of children between 15 and 18, but encourages states to "give priority" to those who are the oldest. In 1999, a strong lobby of NGOs, including AI, tried to persuade the drafters of the Optional Protocol to the Convention on the Rights of the Child to prohibit any recruitment of children under the age of 18. A compromise position was reached, by which only state forces could recruit children between 16 and 18 (armed opposition groups are absolutely forbidden to recruit any child under 18) and only if safeguards are in place to ensure that the child, with his parents or guardians, has given genuine consent (Article 3(3) of the Optional Protocol).

International Labour Organisation (ILO) Convention 182 concerning the Prohibition and Immediate Action for the Elimination of the Worst Forms of Child Labour prohibits the forced or compulsory recruitment of children for use in armed conflict (Article 3(a).

the recruitment of children under 17, and not to deploy anyone under 18 in combat, children as young as 12 reportedly continue to be recruited, sometimes forcibly. For instance, in late 1998, after the LTTE had lost hundreds of cadres in heavy fighting, recruitment was stepped up in areas of the north and east which are largely controlled by the LTTE. A 13-year-old boy from the Muttur area in Trincomalee district, who had been recruited by the LTTE in February 1999 and had twice managed to escape from their camp, was on each occasion forcibly taken back. The second time he was beaten as punishment.

In Nepal, evidence has been mounting that children as young as 14, including girls, are being recruited by members of the armed opposition group, the Communist Party of Nepal (CPN) (Maoist). At least 30 children were abducted in June/July 2000 by members of the CPN (Maoist). Among them are believed to be three 14-year-olds and a 15-year-old from Janapriya High School in Jajarkot district who were reportedly taken from their school hostel in Dashera.

A survey by the Coalition to Stop the Use of Child Soldiers showed that nearly all state armies in Asia recruit under-18s, often flouting their own laws or exploiting legal grey areas. The Coalition has argued that as long as armies are allowed to recruit under-18s, there is no guarantee that they will not end up on the front line. Younger children are serving in the Myanmar armed forces, which recruits large numbers of under-15s, sometimes forcing street children and orphans into its ranks.[67] Many children are also serving in ethnic minority-based armed opposition groups fighting the Myanmar army.

3: TORTURE AT THE HANDS OF THE POLICE

"He had a pair of pliers in his hand. He kept asking where the mobile was. I told him I had not seen it. He then told me to bring my thumb forward. He got hold of my thumb and placed it between the pliers. He pressed it hard and crushed my thumb. I do not remember what happened next."
A nine-year-old boy from Bangladesh describes his treatment by a policeman

Despite the all too evident horrors of armed conflict, it is children suspected of criminal activity — or detained on that pretext — who are most at risk of torture and ill-treatment at the hands of the state. Police officers are responsible for most documented cases of torture; the most common and rapidly increasing form of torture against children is probably the beating of criminal suspects and social marginals in police custody. Beatings can be severe, and even deadly. Children have been struck with fists, sticks, chair legs, gun-butts, whips, iron pipes and electrical cords. They have suffered bruises, concussion, internal bleeding, broken bones, lost teeth and ruptured organs. Children detained by the police have also been sexually assaulted; burned with cigarettes or electricity; exposed to extremes of heat and cold; deprived of food, drink or sleep; or made to stand, sit or hang for long hours in awkward positions. Yet accusations of torture or ill-treatment against law enforcement officials are seldom thoroughly investigated, and even those cases that are prosecuted rarely result in a conviction.

Children in custody

Torture often occurs when the police first apprehend their victim: the abuse may start on the street, in the police car, or under interrogation in police cells. Children are often held without their parents being informed of their whereabouts. This

49

is significant because where children are held without access to relatives or legal counsel, the risk of physical abuse increases dramatically.

In Bangladesh, police kept nine-year-old Firoz in detention, without access to his parents, and tortured him by binding him with rope, hanging him up from a high bar and crushing his thumb with pliers. Firoz, now 10, took months to recover from his physical injuries and is still receiving psychiatric treatment.

Firoz was accused of stealing a mobile telephone while helping a local family to move house. The police came to the boy's home at 3am to arrest him. "They first slapped me on the face, and then pulled my arms down to my sides and tied a rope very tightly over my arms and stomach. It hurt and I could not breathe properly."

Firoz was taken to Mohammadpur Thana Police Station where he was told to squat on the floor. A policeman brought over his chair and sat down facing him: "He lifted his foot and placed his boot on my left knee and began to press it down as hard as he could. My knee was so badly injured that I could not move it. They left me in the cell until the morning. They then came and hung me from a bar. They pulled me up and held my shoulders against the bar and rolled my arms over the bar and left me in that hung position for many hours." The next day, when they still did not have a confession, a policeman crushed Firoz's thumb with a pair of pliers. While the family decided not to file a case against the police for fear of recrimination, the incident was highlighted by both the Bangladesh Rehabilitation Centre for Trauma Victims and the local press. However, the government has failed to bring the perpetrators to justice.

Police officers who are not given adequate training or resources are likely to rely on torture as a method of

Firoz, aged nine, was tortured in Bangladesh when the police detained him for stealing.

© AI

investigation; in some countries the police are encouraged to use coercive methods against criminal suspects in response to high levels of crime. In some cases, the purpose is to extract information, or to obtain a "confession", true or false. In others, punishment and humiliation appear to be the primary aim.

In Morocco, torture and ill-treatment, which had been widespread until the early 1990s, have significantly decreased in recent years. However, reports continue to be received of the practice being used to extract confessions or information, or to punish or intimidate the victims. One 16-year-old student, Hamid Muntassir, said he was blindfolded, repeatedly beaten on the soles of his feet and threatened with electric shocks by police officers. He was held in incommunicado detention for three days in June 1998 on suspicion of killing Mustafa Mansour, a fellow school student, by pushing him off a building.

© Private

Hamid was interrogated at the police station in Azemmour, near Al-Jadida. Hamid told AI: "I explained that we had been studying together and later separated. But the police did not believe me. They accused me of not telling the truth. Then they blindfolded me with a black piece of cloth. They made me sit on the floor. They took off my sandals, lifted my legs and beat me on my bare feet. Later I saw that they had used a black rubber hose to beat me. They told me that I should confess that I had pushed my friend from the building. They beat me several times. They also threatened me with electric shocks."

Hamid Muntassir, a 16-year-old student in Morocco, said he was tortured while being held in incommunicado detention.

The police claim Hamid confessed on the third day of interrogation — signing a testimony by using his thumb. He was brought before the examining magistrate, who noticed he had difficulty standing up and ordered a medical examination. This was not carried out until two weeks later and found no evidence of torture. However, an examination requested by Hamid's lawyer, and carried out a day after the court hearing, noted bruising and swelling on the soles of his feet and that he found it difficult to walk.

A complaint of torture was filed by Hamid's family with the Appeal Court of Al-Jadida, but no public investigation is known to have been carried out. The officers alleged to have tortured Hamid are still on duty. The trial of Hamid Muntassir opened at the beginning of April 1999 and had not concluded by the end of August 2000. The charges against him are based solely on his "confession", which he has since repudiated as it was extracted under torture.

In China, the torture of both criminal suspects and political dissidents is endemic. It takes place in police stations, detention centres, prisons, "re-education through labour" camps and repatriation centres throughout the country. In recent years, officials have even resorted to torture in the collection of fines and taxes and corrupt officials have used it in blackmail and extortion. Many people have been tortured to death. Even very young children are not immune.

China's *Legal Daily* newspaper reported that an eight-year-old boy, Liu Jingjing, was severely beaten during 22 hours in illegal incommunicado detention in Hebei province, Quinglong county. On 1 June 1995, police at the Public Security Bureau (PSB) received a report that the boy might have stolen some money, and a policeman forced his mother to bring the boy to the PSB later that afternoon.

The boy was questioned overnight; his mother was not allowed to be present. He was reportedly beaten, put in thumbcuffs and threatened with being sent to a detention house. By the next morning, he had been forced to "confess" to taking the money. After an equivalent sum was taken from his mother, he was released on bail to await trial. He was dizzy, vomiting and disoriented — all symptoms of head injuries — and a local hospital found evidence of bruising and swelling along the left side of his body. Another hospital later said that "the injured has nervous and mental problems and needs further treatment".

Two weeks later, his mother went to the People's Procuratorate and filed an accusation against the policeman. The police returned the money to her four months later, saying they had no evidence to prove the case against her son. More than two years later, in September 1997, the case against the policeman was heard and Quinglong County Court declared that the policeman had committed the crime of extorting a confession by torture, but was exempt from criminal punishment. The case attracted the attention of legal specialists at the Chinese Political and Legal University, who declared the policeman's exemption from punishment to be without factual or legal basis. It is not known whether the case has been reopened and the policeman punished. A few perpetrators of torture have received heavy prison sentences in recent years, but impunity is the overriding norm. Officials are adept at intimidating witnesses, blocking investigations and exploiting loopholes and ambiguities in the law. Even when a case is investigated, punishment is often lenient.

Rape and sexual abuse

Children in custody, both girls and boys, are vulnerable to rape and sexual abuse. Even the threat of rape — sometimes repeated night after night, while the child sits alone in a dark cell — can cause severe psychological trauma amounting to torture. Rape or sexual abuse, like other forms of torture, may be used to intimidate or humiliate the victim, by demonstrating the absolute power of the torturer over his victim. Rape in custody is not an act of private violence, but a form of torture, for which the state bears responsibility.

The consequences of rape are devastating. Girls who have been raped may be deemed unfit for marriage, which can mean a lifetime of exclusion from social acceptance and economic security. Boys may be labelled weak or unmanly, which could permanently damage their status in their community. Both face the risk of contracting sexually transmitted diseases, including HIV/AIDS, and girls may become pregnant as a result of rape. Many children try to hide the fact that they have been raped, others are simply too embarrassed or ashamed to talk about it; many cases — perhaps most cases — thus go unreported and unpunished. Even when children are willing to make a complaint, and have recourse to the necessary legal advice and assistance, they may be intimidated or pressured not to testify. Children may find it difficult to sustain their allegations, particularly when, as in many cases of sexual violence, there are only two witnesses — the victim and the perpetrator. Moreover, the police assigned to investigate the complaint are often the colleagues of the alleged perpetrator, and police delays or failures to secure medical examinations often means the loss of vital evidence in support of the victim's account.

Testimony of sexual torture has been received from boys and girls as young as 14 in Turkey, who describe being stripped naked, sexually assaulted and threatened with rape. In many cases, the torture testimony of children is supported by medical evidence. Torture in police custody is common in Turkey; children as young as 12 have reportedly been subjected to electric shocks, hosing with cold water and beating.

On separate days in early March 1999, N.C.S., a 16-year-old Kurdish girl,[68] and her 19-year-old friend, Fatma Deniz Polattaş, were arrested and detained at police headquarters in Iskenderun, Turkey, for seven and five days respectively. Both say that they were tortured and forced to give false confessions while in police custody.

According to their testimonies, their torture included rape and other sexual assault. Both were kept blindfolded throughout their detention. For the first two days, N.C.S. was forced to stand continuously, prevented from sleeping and from using the toilet, and denied food and drink except for soured milk. She was forced to strip and remain naked in a cold room. During the interrogation she was beaten — with blows directed especially at her head, genitals, buttocks and breasts — and forced to sit on a wet floor for long periods before being made to roll naked in water. On other occasions she was suspended from the arms and hosed with pressurized cold water. She was threatened that she would be killed and that her mother would be raped. Fatma suffered the same treatment, as well as anal rape with a serrated instrument.

While in police custody the two were seen by state-appointed doctors, including gynaecologists, who performed "virginity tests" without consent. "Virginity tests" are known to be both traumatic and inconclusive, and AI believes that forcibly subjecting detainees to such procedures is an egregious form of gender-based violence constituting torture

© Özgür Bakış

or cruel, inhuman or degrading treatment.

The two young women were remanded to prison on 12 March, and in November 1999 were sentenced to long prison terms after being charged with being members of the armed opposition group Kurdistan Workers' Party (PKK) and taking part in a violent demonstration against the arrest of PKK leader Abdullah Ocalan. They insist that their convictions are based on statements extracted under torture.

Fatma Deniz Pollataş (on the right) and N.C.S. in prison. The young women were reportedly raped, sexually abused and subjected to ill-treatment at police headquarters in Iskenderun, Turkey, in March 1999 when N.C.S. was aged 16.

Following a public outcry and international campaigning, four policemen were put on trial for torture. At the first trial session in April 2000, N.C.S. and Fatma Deniz Pollataş identified three of the police officers. The court decided that the two young women should be examined at a psycho-social trauma centre in Istanbul to find out if they had been sexually abused and ill-treated, but they were not transferred to Istanbul until early June, and not seen until mid-July. As of August 2000, a report on their examination had not yet been prepared and the trial against the four policemen had not reopened. On 29 June, the Appeal Court had upheld the long prison sentences against N.C.S. and Fatma Deniz Polattaş without waiting for the outcome of the trial against the police officers.

A generalized climate of fear and witness intimidation, along with prosecutors' reluctance to investigate the work of security force officers, are among the factors contributing to impunity in Turkey. Even where complaints of serious human rights violations are pursued by the authorities and security officers are prosecuted, only a negligible proportion of them are eventually convicted. According to recent official figures, investigations of 577 security officials accused of torture between 1995 and 1999 resulted in only 10 convictions. In cases where a conviction occurs, security officials often receive the lightest possible sentences.

Deaths in custody

A 1999 Human Rights Watch report found that children detained in Pakistan routinely suffer torture or ill-treatment, including sexual abuse, being beaten, hung upside down, whipped with a rubber strap or specially-designed leather slipper, or held in leg irons.[69] The abuse can be deadly. In May 1998, a 13-year-old boy, Ghulam Jilani, was picked up by police from the northern town of Mansehra. Ghulam, who had already been working as a minibus conductor for three years, was suspected of stealing money from a shop. He was taken to the police station, and later that day a police officer told his family that he had hanged himself in his cell. A boy who had been sharing his cell told a different story – Ghulam had been beaten to death by the police. An autopsy confirmed that Ghulam had died of head injuries. Riots following the boy's funeral prompted provincial authorities to arrest the head constable of the Mansehra police station and order a judicial investigation into the boy's death.[70] No results of the investigation have yet been reported. But this case is the exception; far more often, police abuses against child detainees go unreported and unpunished.

Police in Kenya are similarly able to exploit and abuse any child accused of criminal offences, in any part of the country, with impunity. In May 1997, in the remote northern district of Turkana, 17-year-old Lomurodo Amodoi was arrested by two administration police officers after a stranger accused him of robbery. He was taken to the police station in Lokichokio, where a witness heard him crying out in pain. His body was found two days later in the mortuary in Lodwar, 160 kms away. A police post-mortem failed to establish a cause of death, but relatives insisted that it be repeated; the second post-mortem found that Lomurodo Amodoi had died of strangulation and head injuries. The Turkana District Commissioner told AI delegates visiting Kenya in June 1997 that a police officer had been arrested and charged with the killing. However, he was not in custody and there was no court record of any charge against him. The Attorney General instituted an inquest in November 1997, which has been subject to delays. At the time of writing, two and a half years after his death, the inquest had still not been completed.

In his 1999 report, the Special Rapporteur on torture noted that torture is said to be systematically practised by the security services and police in Egypt. Methods of torture reported included stripping victims, beating with sticks and whips, kicking with boots, electric shocks, suspension from one or both arms, hanging victims by their wrists with their feet touching the floor or forcing them to stand for prolonged hours, dousing them with hot or cold water, and forcing them to stand outdoors in cold weather. Victims are threatened, insulted and humiliated; female victims may be stripped, exposed to verbal and tactile sexual insults, and threatened with rape.[71]

Some people have been tortured to death. Tamer Mohsen 'Ali, aged 17, was reportedly arrested on 14 November 1997 by officers of the Mansoura police station for questioning in connection with a theft. For the next seven days, he was held in police custody, and was reportedly severely beaten and whipped, and given electric shocks to his genitals. He died in custody on 20 November 1997. His body was covered with bruises, and he was found to have a wound to the head and traces of blood in his nose.

In Russia there have also been cases in which children may have been tortured to death. In November 1998, for instance, 17-year-old Vladimir Popov died in hospital, where he had been taken after spending two days in the custody of law enforcement officials in the city of Ekaterinburg. He and a friend had reportedly been arrested on suspicion of theft. According to the friend, police tortured both boys in order to force them to confess. The police authorities claimed that Vladimir jumped out of a window voluntarily, and fell from the third floor of the police department. An autopsy documented numerous injuries on the body, which the family claimed could not have been caused by the alleged fall. A criminal investigation was opened by the Sverdlovsk Regional Office of the Procurator, but was subsequently closed, allegedly for lack of evidence.

Throughout Russia, children in police or correctional custody are subjected to torture and ill-treatment. The authorities' repeated failure to investigate torture allegations properly, much less to charge or convict any of those responsible, has given police and prison officers complete impunity.

The most common methods of torture used in police custody in Russia have been beatings, use of electric shock, and the "elephant" (*slonik*), "swallow"(*lastochka*) and "envelope"(*konvert*) tortures. *Slonik* is reportedly a favoured police method for forcing confessions. The suspect is put in a gas mask and his or her flow of oxygen is restricted or cut off intermittently until the suspect suffocates and agrees to confess. In some cases tear gas has also been forced through the pipe of the gas mask. Some victims have reportedly also been suspended from the ceiling by their arms, which are handcuffed together behind their back.

Abuse by the police is so common that it has become the expected consequence of arrest. One woman told AI that when her young son Dima was arrested on suspicion of theft, she ran after him all the way to the police station "because you know, I had the feeling that they could do anything with him". According to his mother, a nurse, the boy was beaten around the head, had thumbs pressed into his eyeballs, and was kicked and beaten under the ribcage. She waited all day at the station before police

© AI

realized they had the wrong person and decided to let Dima go. "The person who had beaten Dima came up to him, patted him on the shoulder and said: 'Sorry, we made a slight mistake, go home.' They then wrote a certificate for his school explaining where Dima had been all day." The boy added: "They beat me quite severely. It was one person, beating me with his fists, and kicking me with his feet... He just started to beat me — I don't even know what the reason was for it."

Most juveniles awaiting trial in Russia are kept in appalling conditions. Thousands of detainees have no individual beds and have to sleep in shifts. Cells are filthy and insanitary, and illnesses, especially tuberculosis, spread rapidly.

Discriminatory ill-treatment

The torture and ill-treatment of children may sometimes be intensified by discrimination against them because they are poor, or belong to racial or religious minorities. Such victims may also be less likely to receive protection and support from the authorities. Racist abuse has been an element in a number of torture cases investigated by AI.

In Bulgaria, for instance, police brutality against members of the country's 800,000-strong Roma community appears to be endemic. A 1999 survey by the Bulgarian Helsinki Committee concluded that 60 per cent of Roma prisoners alleged they were beaten during arrest or interrogation. Many of the victims of brutal treatment are children.

On 29 April 2000 a 16-year-old Roma boy, Tsvetalin Perov, suffered third degree burns to 15 per cent of his body while in police detention in Vidin. The boy claimed that he had been locked in a room at the police station with a police officer, who beat and kicked him until he passed out. The next thing he remembered was being awoken by the pain of being on fire.

Police say that Tsvetalin Perov set himself on fire. If so, it meant he had a cigarette lighter or matches, and probably would also have needed to douse himself with lighter fuel, as the reported difficulty in extinguishing the fire and the severity of the burns make it likely that a fire accelerant was used. It would be unusual for a suspect to have retained such objects in his possession after the routine search made of any suspect taken into custody by the Bulgarian police. In any event, it remains the responsibility of any arresting authority to take effective steps to ensure that detainees do not harm themselves.

Epileptic and with learning difficulties, Tsvetalin had often been in trouble with the police, and had allegedly been ill-treated before; his sisters recalled several occasions when he returned home from the police station with his clothes covered in blood. In October 1998, a local NGO had filed a complaint about incidents of alleged ill-treatment of Tsvetalin Perov by police officers.

In Switzerland, in November 1999, police officers allegedly beat a 17-year-old Angolan student, "Didier",[72] and subjected him to racist abuse after he was detained on suspicion of having participated in a street fight.

In local media interviews, the boy said that he and two friends witnessed a fight between a man and a woman in the Geneva district of Carouge. One of the friends told the man not to hit the woman, and a struggle ensued. A short while later, according to Didier, the three young men were stopped by a police unit, pinned against a wall and handcuffed.

Didier said that he was thrown to the ground and hit with truncheons before being placed in a police vehicle and taken to Carouge police station. He maintained that during the transfer he was again hit with truncheons and called a "dirty nigger". At the police station, Didier says that he was taken in handcuffs to a cell where he was kicked and subjected to further beatings with truncheons before losing consciousness.

Didier was charged with resisting the police, and was acquitted in January 2000. He had by then filed a complaint against the police, accusing them of causing bodily harm and subjecting him to racist insults. The Attorney General opened a preliminary investigation, and entrusted it to the police under his direction.

In March, while Didier was at school, police searched his family home. Later that month Didier received a summons to report to the police. When he arrived at the station, he was detained and accused of intimidating younger children in order to obtain goods. He was held overnight before being brought before a judge in the Juvenile Court, who instantly dismissed the case against him. Didier's family believes that both incidents were aimed at intimidating him. In April the Attorney General ruled that there were no grounds to justify further investigation into Didier's complaint, and ordered the closure of the dossier. The police had never interviewed Didier himself about his allegations. In August 2000, following an appeal, a Geneva court ruled that an investigating magistrate should carry out a full inquiry into the allegations, including questioning Didier and other relevant witnesses.

Children who remain in police custody after the initial stages of interrogation are often held in police cells — sometimes for months on end — until they are brought before a judge. Such facilities were not intended for children or for long-term occupation. The conditions in police cells are often poor; complaints of inadequate food, medical care, light and air are almost universal. Children detained in police cells generally have no access to recreation, books or exercise areas, and may have to share cells with adults: children confined with adult detainees are in greater danger of sexual or other physical assault.

In Jamaica, a Human Rights Watch report published in July 1999 found that children as young as 12 or 13 were commonly detained for months on end in filthy and overcrowded police lock-ups. The children were often held in the same cells as adults accused of serious crimes, vulnerable to victimization by their cellmates and to ill-treatment by abusive police. Some children detained in cells with adults said they had been beaten, raped, and stabbed by older prisoners. Many children described deliberate physical and mental abuse by the police. One 15-year-old girl told Human Rights Watch that she had been raped by a police officer while held in a lock-up overnight. The lock-ups were dark, fetid and overcrowded; the children had severely limited access to toilets, and were deprived of adequate food, exercise, education, and basic medical care. Some children were locked up only because they were deemed "in need of care and protection", not because they were thought to have committed a criminal offence.[73] A week after the report was published, the government announced that all children would be removed from police lock-ups, and that a new juvenile remand centre would be built within 18 months. Children do continue to be detained for short periods in police cells; in August 2000 AI representatives were told by the Director of Children's Services that children could still be detained for up to a week in police lock-ups while other placements were sought. However, social workers were conducting regular and sometimes unannounced visits to lock-ups in each parish, and were monitoring all cases in which juveniles were held in police custody.

Children in detention in other parts of the Caribbean continue to be held in police lock-ups. In Guyana, a nine-year-old boy was held in the Brickdam lock-up for nearly two months in late 1999 after being accused of stealing an animal. A local newspaper reported that he had been repeatedly sodomized by adult inmates. Previous allegations of sexual abuse of children by adult inmates in Brickdam lock-up had been documented by a national human rights organization.

Abuse of street children

An estimated 100 million children in the world live and work on the streets — begging, peddling fruit, cigarettes or trinkets, shining shoes, often resorting to petty theft and prostitution to survive. Some of them have family links, and return home periodically, but many others have been abandoned, rejected or orphaned, or have run away from home because of abuse or

Lunchtime at Dongri Remand Home in India, Asia's largest remand home for children.

poverty. These children sleep in parks or doorways, under bridges or in abandoned buildings. They are increasingly being targeted by international paedophile and pornography rings. Many are addicted to drugs; in Central America, street children often use inhalants, such as glue, which are cheap and easily accessible, but which cause irreversible brain damage, as well as a host of physical debilities.

Children forced to live on the streets are particularly vulnerable to arbitrary arrest and ill-treatment. Many survive on begging, petty crime or prostitution, activities which bring them regularly to the attention of the police. Some are detained and ill-treated simply because they are easy prey; others are arrested under laws which make destitution, vagrancy and begging criminal offences.

Street children often fall victim to "social cleansing" campaigns, in which local business owners pay to have them chased away or even killed. Many are victims of torture and ill-treatment, and sometimes murder, by police and other authorities. AI has documented violence against street children in many countries, including Bangladesh, Brazil, Colombia, Guatemala, India, Kenya, Nepal and Uganda. What these attacks have in common is the almost complete impunity enjoyed by those who perpetrate them.

Girls on the street are particularly vulnerable to sexual

63

harassment and abuse by the police. In February 1999, for
instance, a uniformed member of the Guatemalan National
Police kicked awake two 15-year-old street children, Lorena
Carmen Hernandez Carranza and Nery Mateo Hernandez, in a
park in Guatemala City. He threw them both to the ground and
told them to take off their clothes, then sexually abused Lorena
for about 20 minutes. The pair identified the officer and lodged
formal complaints with the assistance of a local NGO, Casa
Alianza. After investigating the case, the Guatemalan Human
Rights Ombudsman concluded that the children's human rights
had been violated by the police officer. By September 2000,
however, the officer had not been subject to a criminal
investigation.

Although abuses against street children in Latin America
have been the most thoroughly documented by AI and other
organizations, millions of children in Africa, Asia and Europe
have also been the victims of torture, ill-treatment and other
abuse.

Bangladesh has a large and expanding population of children
who live or work on the streets of the cities, particularly Dhaka.
There are estimates of more than 50,000 street children in
Dhaka alone. These children make a precarious living by
working in odd jobs, in carpet and other textile industries, as
domestic servants or prostitutes; hundreds of children pick over
rubbish dumps for scraps of paper or plastic which can then be
sold. Street children are regularly picked up by the police who
extract bribes, beat, humiliate and harass them. AI has received
numerous reports alleging that children, both male and female,
are sexually abused in custody. Convicted child prisoners are
usually held in wards with adult prisoners, and are known to
have been raped by fellow prisoners and by wardens.
Mohammad Shawkat, a 13-year-old street child, was raped by
two police constables in July 1993 in Dhaka. The next day,
Mohammad was admitted to Dhaka Medical College Hospital
with a bleeding rectum and other injuries. The Assistant
Registrar of the hospital confirmed that the injuries Mohammad
had received were consistent with having been sexually
assaulted. Two Bengali-language newspapers reported the
incident and the two constables were named and suspended,

although it appears that no charges were ever brought against them. Mohammad disappeared from the hospital and could not be located; he may have fled because he feared retaliation or because he was threatened by police.

Some 40,000 street children — among the poorest of the poor — are eking out an existence in Kenya's towns and cities, especially the capital, Nairobi. Street children are harassed and abused by the police, subject to frequent beatings, extortion and sexual abuse; sometimes they are simply rounded up and jailed without cause, or for vagrancy, which is a criminal offence. Girls are often threatened with arrest, and forced to trade sexual favours for freedom. One street girl said: "When the police catch you they ask you for money, or for sex, or else they'll take you to the police station."74 Once in police lock-ups, they face deplorable conditions: often held without toilets, bedding or adequate food and water, they are also likely to be subjected to harassment, ill-treatment or torture. They then face fines or prison terms in one of Kenya's crowded, filthy and often brutal jails. Children are often held with adult prisoners, and have been abused by fellow inmates as well as police and prison guards. In Mombasa, scores of street children have been rounded up by police for sleeping in the streets, and heavily fined or sentenced to a month in jail on charges of causing a public nuisance. These children are detained — and put at risk of torture and ill-treatment in custody — not because they have committed a crime, but simply because they have nowhere else to go. One former street child, tired of being arrested, has taken senior law enforcement officials to the High Court. In September 2000 John Wekesa brought a suit against officials including the police commissioner and the Attorney General, arguing that sleeping in the street was not a crime, and asking for judicial review proceedings to be opened. The court granted leave to take out a judicial review; John Wekesa subsequently went into hiding because of continued police harrassment.

4 : TORTURE OF CHILDREN IN DETENTION

"Life in Panchito is hard. For punishments there were beatings on the soles of the feet or on the palms of the hands, or kicks in the stomach. Boys were stripped naked and hung upside down on the patio and beaten with sticks, or else they made you stand on your hands up against the wall. You had to stay still like that for as long as they wanted, if you fell down they beat you. They'd hang you from a pillar or from the doorway. They hung me up for three hours, and all the guards that passed by hit me. If someone does something and they don't discover who, everyone in the block is beaten with sticks."
A former inmate of the Panchito López juvenile detention centre in Paraguay

Juvenile detention centres

The juvenile detention system in many countries is in crisis — a regime of brutal treatment often goes hand in hand with a rotting infrastructure and an obdurate lack of political will to resolve the situation, or in some cases to even admit that a problem exists. Children awaiting trial may be held for months on end in police lock-ups, often in cells with adults, because there is no juvenile holding facility available. Those moved on to juvenile detention centres to await trial or serve sentences may not fare much better. Children on remand are often held with those who have already been convicted, and inmates are seldom segregated by age or by the seriousness of the charges against them — steps which should be taken to minimize the likelihood of children being abused or influenced by others.

A juvenile held in chains. AI knows of children as young as 10 being made to wear shackles in custody in the USA.

The detention of children ranks low on the list of criminal justice priorities in most countries, so financial resources and government support for improving conditions tend to be limited. Staffing problems are rife, with severe understaffing, lack of training and low pay a feature of juvenile institutions in most parts of the world. Staff are seldom trained in child psychology or specific care issues relating to children, and many view a job in a juvenile facility as a significant step below work with adults. Another widespread problem is that of severe overcrowding; many juvenile facilities regularly hold as much as three times their stated capacity. Guards without adequate training or resources may be responsible for keeping order between dozens of juveniles, and tend to maintain discipline by force.

Children are often detained under conditions that pose a serious threat to their health and safety. Juvenile detention centres are often housed in old and disused adult facilities, with poor heat, light and ventilation; many have no educational or recreational facilities. Conditions are often unsanitary, leaving inmates exposed to disease and other health problems, which can be exacerbated by the often severe overcrowding. Custodial institutions for children seldom have appropriate medical facilities, staff or supplies. In some cases, lack of nourishing food results in malnutrition and, in extreme cases, starvation. Many child detainees are dependent on family members to bring their meals, others have to pay or bribe the authorities just to get adequate and decent food.

Custodial provision for girls in custody is often arbitrary or improvised. Because girls are much less likely to come into contact with the law than boys, their specific needs are rarely taken into consideration. The authorities in many countries have argued that the number of young female offenders is comparatively low, and does not justify the provision of dedicated custodial facilities. As a result girls are more likely to be detained a long way away from their families and to be held together with boys or adults, putting them at risk of sexual abuse and even rape.

> "In Latin America we do not know how many children and youngsters are in prison, or why they are in prison and how they are in the places where they are imprisoned"
> Emilio García Méndez, UNICEF Regional Advisor for Children's Rights.

In some cases, international pressure, often sustained over many years, has forced governments to begin to implement some positive measures. But without the political will to overhaul both an institutionalised culture of violence, as well as the infrastructure that supports it, reforms are often cosmetic, incomplete and ultimately ineffective.

La Correccional de Menores "Panchito López": "Panchito López" juvenile detention centre in Asunción, Paraguay, is a byword for ill-treatment and wretched conditions. After an on-site visit to Paraguay in July 1999, the Inter-American Commission on Human Rights (IACHR) said: "The dire conditions faced by detainees in Paraguay are common knowledge... However, the IACHR cannot fail to mention that the most serious problems it detected were at Panchito López..[75]

The Paraguayan government has long been promising to close down Panchito López. In October 1999, AI delegates were assured by the Vice-Minister of Justice that transfer of the inmates to a new, purpose-built, juvenile detention centre was "imminent". The IACHR received similar assurances, and was told explicitly that Panchito López would be relocated by the end of 1999. As of September 2000, the facility remains open.

Ill-treatment, sometimes amounting to torture, is endemic in Panchito López. On 25 February 2000, for instance, prison guards reportedly left Francisco Carballo Figueredo, aged 15, upside down and manacled to a column for several hours in the early morning sun. Witnesses who saw him afterwards said his back was badly bruised from a beating, and that he showed signs of severe anxiety and stress. On the same day another inmate, 17-year-old Rubén Dario Alcaraz, was reportedly hung up by his wrists and kicked by guards wearing steel toe-capped boots.

Over the years, there has been a steady stream of allegations about physical punishments amounting to torture or

© Gustavo Gaona

A boy who escaped from a burning cell block is watched over by a guard at Panchito López juvenile detention centre in Paraguay, February 2000. Eight boys died in the fire or shortly afterwards and a further 20 sustained permanent injuries.

cruel, inhuman or degrading treatment; including boys being kicked, beaten, suspended upside down, having plastic bags put over their heads, being beaten on the back with a hammer or having their hands and feet scalded. Some reported being denied food, drink, or access to toilets — sometimes for several days. There appears to be a high incidence of random brutality from the prison guards: If a guard calls your name, one boy explained, "he's looking for you to punish you. It's worse if you don't go along. You go, you hold your hands up, you let them beat you." A Paraguayan newspaper noted that some boys had been threatened by the guards, and warned not to testify in one of the few cases of ill-treatment under investigation.[76]

The conditions in which the boys are held themselves amount to cruel, inhuman and degrading treatment. The Panchito López facility in Asunción was converted into a detention centre from a private home; it is desperately overcrowded. "Panchito López currently has 270 inmates in a space suited to a maximum of 80," said the facility's Director, Melitón Bittar, in February 2000. "The overcrowding is terrible, it's an undeniable reality."

The overwhelming majority of the inmates have not been tried or convicted of any crime.[77] Many spend months or even years awaiting trial, in filthy and severely overcrowded cells with few toilets or washing facilities. Temperatures in the cell blocks can hover at around 40°c (100°F) for days on end. In some dormitories, the inmates have to sleep three to a bed; a journalist who visited the facility noted that each child got about the same amount of personal space "as that covered by a newspaper". Inmates are not segregated by age or offence: aggressive boys, timid ones, tough repeat offenders, convicted drug dealers and suspected shoplifters are all crammed in together.

"Many use drugs," a former inmate said, "because it's very hard to be locked up, always seeing the same faces. Sometimes you don't care if you live or die. At the beginning it's more difficult. The guards will sell you marijuana and many do deals with them ... they can also get you pills and alcohol."

On 11 February 2000, inmates of cell eight apparently set their dormitory on fire in protest at the constant barrage of ill-treatment, particularly a severe beating by two of the guards on

several of the cell's occupants the night before.[78] Survivors say
that guards refused to open the cell doors to allow the more
than 30 inmates to escape the flames until reinforcements
arrived. Two boys died in the blaze, and another five would die
slowly over the next few days. An eighth victim lingered in
hospital for several months. More than 20 suffered third-degree
burns, leaving many of them permanently disfigured.

After a second fire broke out a week later, some 25 juveniles
were transferred to the Emboscada prison, an adult facility,
known to be damp and vermin-infested, without adequate light
or ventilation and containing no enclosed toilet facilities. They
are only allowed out for recreation for between 30 minutes and
one hour per day, and there are no medical, educational or
social services. Several boys have complained of severe beatings
and other ill-treatment, and at least 13 were apparently put in
incommunicado detention in an isolation cell in the adult
pavilion.

In May the *Centro de Educación Integral* was finally opened
in Itauguá, about 25 km from Asunción; it is a purpose-built
juvenile detention centre, on nine hectares of land, with its
own vegetable gardens, classroom, football fields, volleyball
courts and other recreation spaces. Yet the new facility only
has a capacity of about 160 to 180, hardly enough to absorb the
population of Panchito López and allow it to be closed, as the
government has long promised. By the end of September only
about 120 boys had been transferred to the *Centro*, mostly
those the authorities considered to be "the good ones". New
buildings alone cannot solve the problem of an entrenched
culture of violence within the juvenile detention system. Boys
have apparently been returned to Panchito López as a
disciplinary measure, while one of the punishments for
misbehaviour at Panchito López is rumoured to be a transfer to
Emboscada prison. Meanwhile, about 150 inmates remain in
the old Panchito López building in Asunción, where the loss of
the fire-damaged cells has intensified the problem of
overcrowding. There has been no reported let-up in the
endemic ill-treatment.

The young inmates of juvenile detention centres across
Brazil face similarly horrendous conditions. Torture, ill-

treatment and cruel, inhuman and degrading conditions —
including extraordinary levels of overcrowding — are endemic.
Facilities are chronically understaffed, and the few existing staff
are untrained, underpaid and prone to using violence to control
the dozens of boys they may be charged with supervising.
Punishments are arbitrary, meted out at the whim of warders
(known as *monitores*), and often deliberately designed to
humiliate. Several boys have died following beatings by
monitores. Collective punishments are common — if one boy
breaks a rule, many boys are punished.

In São Paulo state, conditions have gone from bad to worse.
The state's juvenile detention system, Foundation for the Well-
Being of Minors (FEBEM), collapsed into crisis in October 1999
after years of brutality and overcrowding had sparked off a series
of violent riots. Even the warders admit that violence against
inmates is the norm in FEBEM's detention centres.

In mid-1999, FEBEM's Imigrantes complex, built with a
capacity of 360, was housing 1,648 inmates. The boys — many of
whom were suffering from skin and respiratory diseases — slept
three to a bed; those spilling over from the dormitories slept
sitting up, in the corridors and even in the filthy bathrooms. Ten
to 15 *monitores* were expected to oversee an average of 350
detainees — maintaining discipline by beating the children with
clubs and metal rods. Inmates have described the practice of
repique — slang at Imigrantes for revenge lashings — which
involved marching inmates outside in their underwear, tucking
their heads between their knees and striking them repeatedly on
their backs.

On the night of 11 September 1999, boys in one wing of
Imigrantes rioted, set fire to part of the wing, and took some of
the *monitores* hostage. Televised news reports showed dozens of
boys running across the prison yard, pursued by *monitores* —
some of whom were hooded wielding sticks. *Monitores* were
filmed running over crouched and naked boys, kicking, punching
and beating them with sticks. Some 650 boys managed to escape.

A further riot on 24 October 1999 was even more brutal.
Rioting teenagers armed with clubs and bricks overtook the
Imigrantes compound; the boys took hostages, burned

©TV Globo Ltda

These two photos reflect the shocking state of São Paulo's juvenile detention system. (Above) Boys in B wing at the recently closed FEBEM Imigrantes are rounded up and beaten by wardens during a riot, 11 September 1999. (Below) Boys in their cell in FEBEM Santo André Systematic torture, extreme overcrowding and appalling conditions have brought the juvenile detention system in São Paulo to near collapse.

© Private

mattresses and injured fellow detainees, killing four of them with a brutality that shocked even those who had worked in the system for years. An additional 58 people were injured, including 29 FEBEM staff, dozens of boys escaped, and the Imigrantes complex was completely destroyed. Some 16 *monitores* were taken hostage and beaten.

After the riots, the authorities began to transfer young inmates into higher security adult penal facilities. On 24 November 1999, for instance, 405 boys were transferred by military police riot troops to Santo André public jail. Many of the detainees allege that upon arrival they were taught "the rules of the house" by being forced to run a gauntlet of *monitores*, who beat them with iron bars and sticks. They were also forced to sit on the floor stripped to their underpants while they were kicked and beaten on the head. They were then made to take cold showers to reduce the appearance of bruising. Medical examinations of 95 boys, made two days after the transfer, showed that only 16 of them did not bear the marks of beatings.

In São Paulo's largest remaining facility, the Tatuapé complex, a riot broke out in the Therapeutic Referral Unit on 19 February 2000; inmates claimed that the unit was being used as a torture chamber, referred to as the "dungeon". Public prosecutors called after the riot found that boys were wearing only underpants and were being held four to five in tiny cells containing only one concrete bed. They were allowed out of these cells for only 30 minutes a day. Boys claimed that beatings were carried out mainly at night by a group of *monitores* from different units of the complex, referred to as the "ninjas". Members of this group dressed entirely in black and covered their faces with balaclavas.

In May 2000, Tatuapé complex, still suffering severe overcrowding with a population of 1,200 adolescents, once again descended into a spate of riots, and riot troops were called in to take control. A number of boys fled in the chaos, and a police commander alleged that they had been let out by FEBEM staff. Riots broke out again on 11 June 2000, during which a female *monitor* was reportedly thrown from the roof by inmates, breaking both legs.

The São Paulo government has refused to acknowledge the human rights violations underlying the FEBEM crisis; their solution has been to launch a program to build more high security detention facilities, a process which neither solves the problems in hand nor addresses the fundamental issues at the heart of the crisis. The situation in São Paulo state is extreme, but conditions in youth detention centres across Brazil are similarly failing to live up to the standards promised by the country's *Estatuto da Criança e do Adolescente* (ECA), the Statute of the Child and Adolescent, which celebrated its 10th anniversary in June 2000. The ECA is a highly progressive piece of legislation for the protection of children, but without the political will to turn its words into action, it provides little remedy to the thousands of children being tortured and ill-treated in Brazil's juvenile justice system.

Conditions of detention in Pakistan are likewise deplorable, often amounting to cruel, inhuman or degrading treatment; children may spend as long as three months in police custody before they even see a judge for the first time. Once charged, they typically spend more months, or even years, in custody, waiting for their cases to be concluded. In February 1998, there were some 2,700 juvenile prisoners in Punjab province alone; only 10 per cent of whom had been convicted of any crime. The situation of those who spend extended periods on remand is all the more appalling because the vast majority are eventually found not guilty by the courts — the conviction rate for children is between 13 and 17 per cent. Although prisons in Pakistan's major cities have segregated wards for juveniles, children are housed with adults in many of the country's smaller jails and many have to depend on their families to bring them food. Children are frequently subjected to sexual abuse by adult inmates and by prison guards, who have also been accused of supplying illegal drugs. Medical care is rudimentary, and the Human Rights Commission of Pakistan noted in 1996 that denial of medical care is often used as a form of punishment.[79]

Cruel, inhuman and degrading conditions in juvenile detention centres are not confined to countries of the South: many of AI's recent cases, including the cruel use of force and restraints, come from the USA and there have also been cases from Western Europe, including the UK. In March 1999, the UK's Chief Inspector of Prisons condemned the treatment and conditions of the country's largest young offender institution and remand centre, housing some 900 inmates, as "unacceptable in a civilised country". He also said the "core of the institution is rotten". Inspectors found young prisoners in Feltham Institution who were locked up for 22 hours a day in "cold, dilapidated and dirty cells". Many had no blankets, "pitifully inadequate" personal clothing and unwashed bedlinen. Some prisoners had no exercise or access to fresh air.[80] Although an inspection in late 1999 seemed to suggest that some reforms were under way, the deputy governor of the prison resigned in August 2000 in protest at conditions, referring to the prison regime as "Dickensian".

In the USA, children have been held in cruel conditions in overcrowded facilities, where they have also been deprived of adequate mental health care, education, and rehabilitation programs. Some have been subjected to brutal force and cruel punishments, including shackles, chemical sprays and electro-shock devices. Solitary confinement is also a common punishment in juvenile facilities in the USA, in violation of international standards. In March 2000, the US Justice Department sought an emergency court order to stop ill-treatment of children at the Jena Juvenile Justice Center in Louisiana. Children held there were routinely subjected to excessive force and prolonged isolation, and deprived of shoes, blankets and medical care. Chemical agents were also abused. In November 1999 a CS gas grenade, designed for outdoor use, was used in a dormitory containing 46 children. The children fled outside where they were made to lie face down on concrete, some only in their underwear, for hours. Several were allegedly sprayed in the face with mace while on the ground. The memorandum in support of the injunction noted that "penal officers at Jena have rubbed inmates' faces into cement floors, taken away clothing, slammed youths against doors, walls, and floors, and forced naked juveniles to squat with their buttocks in the air while searches are performed ... evidence exists showing officers actually have encouraged peer violence." Mentally disabled juveniles were placed in isolation as a punitive

measure; some were punished for trying to commit suicide. A
federal judge ordered the immediate removal of several boys
who had been severely ill-treated from the centre, including a
15-year-old who had repeatedly attempted suicide.

In December 1999, the Governor of Maryland moved to
suspend the state's juvenile boot camps after allegations of
serious ill-treatment of the children held in them. Guards
reportedly used verbal abuse, excessive force, restraints
including leg shackles, and other intimidatory practices. The
Baltimore Sun newspaper, whose reporter spent five months at
the Savage Leadership Challenge boot camp, said: "It's routine
for guards to bust a 15-year-old boy's lip. To bloody noses. To
slam kids to the ground and crash down on them with full force
for little or no reason."

In South Dakota, a class action lawsuit was filed on 24
February 2000 on behalf of children held in the State Training
School in Plankinton. It alleged, *inter alia*, that children were
subjected to four-point restraint procedures in which they were
forced to lie on their backs, spread-eagled, on a raised concrete
bed in an isolation cell. Their wrists and ankles were then
handcuffed and shackled to rings embedded in the concrete.
Children were reportedly held in this position for hours at a
time, including overnight; girls held in this position had been
stripped naked by male staff, sometimes having their clothes cut
off with scissors. It was also alleged that children were routinely
held in isolation for 23 hours a day, sometimes for months at a
time. This is of particular concern given that a number of
children in Plankinton reportedly suffered from mental illness.
In July 1999, a 14-year-old girl inmate had died after an enforced
running exercise.

Children held with adults

Children held in adult prisons and housed with adult inmates
have frequently been the target of sexual and physical abuse by
adult inmates, and are at greater risk of suicide. Recognizing
this, international standards expressly state that incarcerated
children should be separated from adult inmates. In many
countries, however, children are routinely housed with adults.

In the USA, for instance, AI found that at the end of 1998, 40 states were holding at least 3,700 children in adult prisons without segregation from adult inmates.

Boys are vulnerable to sexual abuse from adult male prisoners, which can sometimes put their lives at risk. In Malawi, for instance, some prison wardens are reported to have been bribed to smuggle boys into adult cell blocks for sex. "These juveniles agreed to have sex with these men because they have no clothes, no blanket, and they were hungry," said one adult prisoner. "One day these boys started to cry and refused to have sex. The men took away their blankets and after spending a night in the cold they agreed to allow the men to have sex with them again. We try to tell these boys that they will die of AIDS, but what can these boys do? They have nothing..."

A study into HIV/AIDS in Malawi's prisons, commissioned by the chief

Children crammed into the compound at Zomba Central Prison, Malawi. Prison warders were found to have been bribed to smuggle boys into adult cell blocks for sex.

© Penal Reform International

commissioner of prisons and carried out by Penal Reform International, discovered that young boys are being recruited into well-established prostitution rings or forced into giving sexual favours to older inmates. Some prison officers are reported to act as go-betweens, smuggling boys into adult blocks for as little as 30 US cents to supplement their meagre incomes. In two Malawi prisons, Maula and Chichiri, medical assistants report that nearly all inmates with peri-anal abscesses are under 18 years old. HIV and AIDS is rife, with little done to prevent the spread of the virus or to treat patients already infected.

As of August 2000, more than 140 boys aged between 12 and 18 were being held in Zomba Central Prison, the largest in the country. Most were awaiting trial, while others were serving prison sentences, some for minor offences such as stealing food. The prison is filthy, unhygienic, overcrowded and underfunded; many of the boys held there are hungry, and have no blankets or clothing beyond what they are wearing when they arrive. Although boys are supposed to be kept apart from adults in Malawi's prisons, they can come into contact, for instance, in the kitchen, the library and on work detail. At Zomba, the most common way of smuggling boys into adult blocks is through the clinic, which is used by both adults and children. "An adult prisoner approaches a prison officer, gives him some money and asks him to get him a boy. You know some prisoners are rich compared to the guards. The guard then smuggles a juvenile into the adult blocks when they are out of the juvenile wing. Once they are there they can be hidden for months, and the man who paid for them rents them out to other prisoners 'for short time', using other prisoners to get him customers."

Homosexuality is illegal in Malawi. It is therefore unlikely that the prison authorities will acknowledge that sexual violence is happening on a large scale inside the prisons. Because the authorities do not fully admit that the problem exists, they take little action to protect the boys, leaving them vulnerable to further abuse, as well as to HIV infection and other sexually transmitted diseases. As the HIV/AIDS epidemic continues unabated in Sub-Saharan Africa — with 23 million people already HIV positive — prisons have become fertile grounds for transmission of the disease. Of the 167 deaths in Malawi prisons during 1997, 40 per cent were attributed to AIDS. In a six-month period during 1998, 49 per cent of all prisoners who visited the clinic at Zomba Central Prison were found to be HIV positive. Prisoners believe that sufferers die faster in prison because of the poor diet and living conditions.

Cruel, inhuman or degrading treatment in other institutions

Orphans and abandoned children
States also have custody of large numbers of children in non-penal custodial institutions, including orphanages and foster care centres. Children in orphanages or state homes often have at least one living parent, but have been abandoned because of poverty, or because a parent is ill or in jail. Many children are institutionalized after being taken away from an abusive or incompetent parent. In countries with restrictive population control policies, or where cultural traditions value boys highly, girls are more likely to be abandoned. In some cases, children born with disabilities are abandoned at birth, while even healthy children given up for financial or domestic reasons are often assumed to be "defective".[81] Orphanages and other state-run institutions suffer from many of the same structural problems that beset juvenile justice facilities, including under-funding, poorly trained and underpaid staff, and an overall lack of resources. Institutions regarded as social services are generally accorded a lower priority and tend to receive less state funding than prisons and detention centres. Yet children in orphanages, like children in custody, are often subjected to cruel, inhuman and degrading conditions, and many suffer deadly levels of abuse and neglect.

In early 2000 two children reportedly died as a result of extreme neglect in the state-run Dzhurkovo home for mentally handicapped children in Bulgaria. Four-year-old Galya reportedly had acute double bronchial pneumonia for two weeks prior to her death, yet the administrators of the home did not refer her to a hospital. Rosen Nanev, aged 13, is also reported to have died of bronchial pneumonia. In 1997 AI had

©Reuters/Popperfoto

written to President Stoyanov expressing concern about seven children who had died of malnutrition and hypothermia while they were wards in the home between 31 January and 27 February 1997. Nine-year-old Angelina Atanasova, who died on 25 February, reportedly weighed only seven kilograms, while 18-year-old Diana Dechkova, who died two days later, reportedly weighed 11 kilograms. Roughly 20 per cent of the children in the home were bed-ridden or otherwise immobilized, with little protection from the severe cold. Such extreme neglect clearly constitutes a form of torture or severe cruel, inhuman or degrading treatment. According to the Bulgarian Helsinki Committee, the average level of food provision budgeted for each child in state-run children's homes is 45 stotinki (0.45 deutschmarks) per day, and in most cases provision is only kept at a minimum level by aid and charitable donations.

Dangerously low levels of food and other provisions reportedly occur where children's homes are geographically isolated, or where the administrators of a home are insufficiently active in soliciting outside donations.

A Russian child sits on the floor of a psycho-neurological institution in Moscow. A 1998 Human Rights Watch report documented extraordinary levels of cruelty and neglect in the treatment of children abandoned to the state, who number more than 100,000 each year.

Children in state orphanages may also be vulnerable to potentially dangerous exploitation. In a case in Bulgaria in May 2000, a psychologist conducted an experiment with a psychotropic drug on 15 children in the Maria Teresa orphanage in Stara Zagora. Three children were briefly hospitalized after taking Rispolept, a drug intended to control aggression in schizophrenics. The 15 children, who were not known to be schizophrenic, were asked to fill out a questionnaire by the psychologist, who appeared to be conducting research on behalf of a professor of the medical faculty of Thrace University. The incident is being investigated. The Law on Drugs and Pharmacies, adopted in January 2000, includes a provision which allows drug experiments to be conducted on orphans if a court order is obtained, although it does not appear that a court order was applied for in this case.

In China, a 1996 Human Rights Watch study found evidence of a pattern of cruelty, abuse, and malign neglect that resulted in mortality rates in state-run children's institutions of up to 90 per cent. The Chinese government challenged the study, but even their own statistics demonstrated that a child admitted to an orphanage had less than a 50 per cent chance of surviving their first year; in some provinces the likelihood of survival dropped to one in 10. Eyewitness accounts and medical records from China's best-known and most prestigious orphanage, the Shanghai Children's Welfare Institute, revealed that orphans were deliberately starved, tortured and sexually assaulted, leading to the unnatural deaths of well over 1,000 children between 1986 and 1992 alone. Child-care workers reportedly selected unwanted infants and children for death by intentional deprivation of food and water — a process known among the workers as the "summary resolution" of children's alleged medical problems.[82] The report suggests that these abuses occurred as a result of state policy — an allegation given some credence by the Chinese government's inadequate response when the case provoked international outcry, and by their reported cover-up of a lengthy internal investigation.

In Russia, children have been abandoned to the state at a rate of more than 100,000 per year. In a 1998 report, Human Rights Watch documented extraordinary levels of cruelty and neglect in the treatment of some of these children, most of whom have at least one living parent. The report makes harrowing reading. It alleges that a large number of the infants relegated to state institutions are classified as disabled and sent to "lying-down" rooms, where they are occasionally changed and fed but are otherwise left to their own devices. With no human contact, no one to play with or to cuddle, and no visual or aural stimulation, any disability these babies may have suffered at birth is intensified; many of those who survive such an infancy are left unable to function or to communicate. If they do live to the age of four, they are evaluated. Those labelled severely "retarded" are condemned to a lifetime in locked and isolated "psycho-neurological internats", where they are similarly deprived of stimulation and medical treatment. They may be restrained in cloth sacks, or left tethered to a bed or other piece of furniture; they are seldom bathed or fed properly. Children classed as "normal" are also subjected to brutal treatment in state-run orphanages, including beatings, sexual abuse, being locked in freezing rooms for days at a time, or in one case being thrown out of a high window while locked in a small wooden chest. Older children are often encouraged to beat up, bully, and intimidate younger ones. Children have no means of redress or complaint to protest against ill-treatment and abuse at the hands of staff and older children.[83]

Corporal punishment

In some countries, children can be sentenced by a court to corporal punishment, most commonly flogging. The sentence is often carried out in public, and can cause severe pain and suffering, as well as permanent injury. Some children have been sentenced to hundreds of lashes.

In Nigeria, women and girls who have been raped may be unable to obtain justice and may be deterred from reporting offences for fear of being punished themselves. Punishments include public floggings. In early September 2000 Bariya Ibrahim Magazu, aged 17, was sentenced to 180 strokes of the cane in Zamfara State, northern Nigeria. She had no legal representation and was unable to produce witnesses to substantiate her claim that three men had sexual relations with her, and that one had made her pregnant. She was sentenced to 100 lashes for having sexual relations outside marriage and a further 80 lashes for her accusations against the three men, which were judged to be false. The sentence was not due to be carried out until at least 40 days after the delivery of her baby, expected in November. In February 2000 Zuweira Aliyu, aged 16, was sentenced to 100 lashes, also in Zamfara State. The sentence was reportedly not carried out because she was suffering from ill-health. The young man convicted with her, 18-year-old Sani Mamman, was publicly flogged shortly after conviction.

The Nigerian Federal Government has advised citizens whose constitutional rights have been violated in state courts to seek legal redress in the higher courts, including the Supreme Court. However, sentences are often carried out immediately after conviction and most defendants have no means to bring an appeal.

In Saudi Arabia on 25 March 1996 — just one month after the Children's Convention had come into force in the country — AI received reports that two pupils were flogged after being convicted of assaulting a teacher. Nasir al-Shibani and Muhammad Majed al-Shibani, from al-Thaqueef Secondary School in Taif, were respectively sentenced to 210 and 150 lashes in addition to three and two months' imprisonment. Part of their flogging was carried out before other pupils and teachers at the school.

RECOMMENDATIONS

Governments are obliged under international law to respect and to ensure the right of children to be free from torture and ill-treatment under all circumstances. A state's obligation does not end when it ratifies the Convention on the Rights of the Child, or passes legislation outlawing the torture of children. Moreover, non-governmental groups must also take measures to protect children and prevent torture. The recommendations that follow have been drafted with a view towards providing practical steps aimed at ending the torture of children including by improving protection, holding governments and opposition groups accountable, implementing preventative safeguards, prosecuting torturers, and addressing underlying causes and contributing factors, such as discrimination.

1. Governments should clearly and unequivocally condemn the torture of children whenever it occurs. They must make clear to all members of the security forces and judiciary that torture must never be tolerated. The leaders of armed political groups must likewise make clear to their forces that torture is always unacceptable.

2. Torture should be expressly prohibited in law, in line with the UN Convention on the Rights of the Child, the UN Convention against Torture and other international standards. States should also ensure that their laws do not facilitate, condone or allow impunity for acts by private individuals that may amount to torture, and should take measures to ensure that such laws are enforced.

RECOMMENDATIONS FOR THE PROTECTION OF CHILDREN IN ARMED CONFLICT

3. Governments and armed political groups should expressly prohibit the torture or ill-treatment of children, and emphasize to members of their forces that anyone who commits or tolerates the torture or ill-treatment of children will be held strictly accountable.

4. Governments and armed political groups should reiterate to members of their forces that there is no defence of superior orders.

5. Governments and armed political groups should instruct members of their forces to end rape, sexual abuse and other forms of torture or ill-treatment of captured children, and should make a public commitment to observing international humanitarian law standards prohibiting torture, in particular the Protocol Additional to the Geneva Conventions of 1949, and relating to the Protection of Victims of Non-International Armed Conflicts (Protocol II).

6. Governments and armed political groups should immediately remove any combatant suspected of committing torture from situations where such abuses might recur.

7. Governments and armed political groups should ensure that children are not held as hostages or detained in place of their parents or other family members.

8. Governments and armed political groups should take all measures to protect children from rape and other forms of sexual violence, including by instructing all combatants to respect international humanitarian law and to end rape and other forms of sexual violence immediately.

9. Governments should investigate all reports of rape and other forms of sexual violence by combatants under their control and prosecute those alleged to have committed these offences. Armed political groups should likewise investigate all allegations of rape and sexual violence against combatants under their control, and hold them strictly accountable.

10. Governments and armed political groups should state publicly that rape and other forms of torture in the conduct of armed conflict constitutes a war crime, and that anyone who commits such a crime will be held accountable.

11. The rights of refugee and internally displaced children, including protection against recruitment and sexual exploitation, should be respected. Displaced people should be given support to exercise their right of return, or to resettle in safety and dignity.

CHILD SOLDIERS

12. Governments and armed political groups should publicly condemn and prohibit the recruitment and use of child soldiers; should immediately cease the forcible, compulsory or voluntary recruitment and use of children under the age of 18; and should disarm, demobilize and reintegrate all child soldiers.
13. Governments should take prompt and effective measures to ensure that no child under the age of 18 is recruited for military service, including by passing legislation raising the minimum age for military recruitment to 18.
14. Governments should ratify without delay the Optional Protocol to the Convention on the Rights of the Child on the Involvement of Children in Armed Conflict.

RECOMMENDATIONS FOR THE PROTECTION OF CHILDREN IN CUSTODY

15. Governments should state publicly that any form of torture, ill-treatment or other physical abuse of children by law enforcement officials will not be tolerated.
16. Police authorities should notify the parent or guardian immediately when a child is detained unless this would endanger the child's safety.
17. The child's right to legal counsel, to have their legal counsel present during interrogation, and to have unrestricted and private access to their legal counsel should be respected.
18. Other basic procedural safeguards such as the presumption of innocence, the right to remain silent and the right of a child to have access to a parent or guardian should also be respected at all stages of the proceedings.
19. No child should ever be held in secret or incommunicado detention.
20. All law enforcement officials should receive training on the special needs and rights of children in custody.
21. Statements extracted from a child under torture or ill-treatment should not be admissible as evidence in any proceedings against the child. Such statements should only be used as evidence against the person accused of torture or ill-treatment.

22. The policies and practices of law enforcement agencies on the protection of children in detention should conform to relevant standards, especially the Convention on the Rights of the Child and the United Nations Rules for the Protection of Juveniles Deprived of their Liberty.

23. All allegations of torture or abuse by law enforcement officials should be investigated promptly, the methods and results of the investigations should be made public, and the perpetrators brought swiftly to justice.

24. All investigations into possible cases of torture by law enforcement officials should be carried out promptly, impartially, independently and thoroughly, and not by the suspect's immediate colleagues. Children should have secure access to an independent mechanism for lodging allegations of torture or ill-treatment.

25. Law enforcement agencies should be subject to independent supervision, by a body having an automatic right of access to any place where children are detained, especially police stations, and with the power to report publicly on its findings.

26. All children in custody should have access to medical care and to facilities for the prevention and treatment of illness; girls in custody should have access to a female doctor or nurse.

27. The use of pre-trial detention for children should be limited to exceptional circumstances, and all forms of detention should be consistent with the international standard that children should only be detained as a last resort and for the shortest possible period of time.

28. Children in custody should be separated from adults, unless they are members of the same family.

29. Girls should be held separately from boys, and should be supervised by female members of staff.

30. Children detained pending a court's decision should be separated from those already convicted of an offence and should also be separated by age, seriousness of offence and physical size.

31. Appropriate measures should be taken to protect all children in custody from rape and sexual abuse, recognizing that girls

are particularly vulnerable to these forms of torture and ill-treatment.

32. All forms of corporal punishment and physical abuse of children should be strictly prohibited. Staff found to have subjected children to corporal punishment or other abuse should be removed from contact with children immediately and subjected to disciplinary action, as well as criminal charges where appropriate.

33. The authorities should ensure that torture or ill-treatment in custody, as well as failure to report misconduct by law enforcement officials or correctional staff, will not be tolerated, and that those found involved in such abuses will be adequately disciplined or criminally prosecuted.

34. The staff of juvenile detention facilities should undergo psychological assessments and background checks to ensure that they are suitable for work with children, and should be adequately trained in the special needs and rights of child detainees.

CRUEL, INHUMAN AND DEGRADING CONDITIONS OF DETENTION

35. No child should be held in conditions that pose a serious risk to their life or health, including severe overcrowding, lack of adequate food and drink, lack of proper sanitation, exposure to extremes of heat or cold, exposure to infectious diseases and denial of medical care.

36. Children should not be subjected to physical restraint devices except in exceptional cases, where all other control methods have been exhausted and failed. The use of dangerous and cruel restraint procedures by law enforcement officials and staff of custodial institutions — such as hogtying and choke holds — should be banned.

37. The use of electro-shock stun belts on children should be prohibited.

38. Corporal punishment, placement in a dark cell, enforced isolation, withholding of food, and denial of access to family visits should be prohibited.

39. Children suffering from mental illness should not be held in juvenile detention centres.

RECOMMENDATIONS FOR THE PROTECTION OF CHILDREN IN SCHOOLS

40. The use of corporal punishment in all schools, public and private, should be abolished.
41. Programs should be established to educate parents, teachers and society at large about the harm of corporal punishment in schools and the existence of effective alternatives.
42. Governments must take appropriate disciplinary action against teachers found to have violated the prohibition on corporal punishment, as well as initiating criminal prosecution where appropriate.
43. Education programs should be established to teach children about their human rights, including the right to be free from cruel, inhuman or degrading treatment or punishment, as well as other rights enshrined in international human rights instruments, including the Convention on the Rights of the Child.

RECOMMENDATIONS FOR THE PROTECTION OF CHILDREN IN OTHER INSTITUTIONS

44. Governments should ensure that the human rights of all abandoned and orphaned children are fully respected, and that they are protected from discrimination, including discriminatory ill-treatment.
45. Governments should ensure that children are only placed in orphanages or other custodial institutions if it is in the best interests of the child to do so.
46. Governments should ensure that the corporal or other abusive punishment of children in state-run institutions is strictly prohibited.
47. The authorities should reiterate that any staff member alleged to have ill-treated children in care will be subject to investigation and if appropriate, will be disciplined, dismissed or submitted to criminal prosecution.

48. All state-run residential institutions should be subject a
    system of regular inspections by an independent body which
    should be composed of professionals from relevant fields,
    and which should have automatic rights of access to the
    institution, as well as the power to make recommendations
    and report publicly on its findings.

Appendix: AI's 12-Point Program for the Prevention of Torture by Agents of the State

Amnesty International

12-Point Program for the Prevention of Torture by Agents of the State

Torture is a fundamental violation of human rights, condemned by the international community as an offence to human dignity and prohibited in all circumstances under international law.

Yet torture persists, daily and across the globe. Immediate steps are needed to confront torture and other cruel, inhuman or degrading treatment or punishment wherever they occur and to eradicate them totally.

Amnesty International calls on all governments to implement the following 12-Point Program for the Prevention of Torture by Agents of the State. It invites concerned individuals and organizations to ensure that they do so. Amnesty International believes that the implementation of these measures is a positive indication of a government's commitment to end torture and to work for its eradication worldwide.

1. Condemn torture
The highest authorities of every country should demonstrate their total opposition to torture. They should condemn torture unreservedly whenever it occurs. They should make clear to all members of the police, military and other security forces that torture will never be tolerated.

2. Ensure access to prisoners
Torture often takes place while prisoners are held incommunicado — unable to contact people outside who could help them or find out what is happening to them. The practice of incommunicado detention should be ended. Governments should ensure that all prisoners are brought before an independent judicial authority without delay after being taken

into custody. Prisoners should have access to relatives, lawyers and doctors without delay and regularly thereafter.

3. No secret detention

In some countries torture takes place in secret locations, often after the victims are made to "disappear". Governments should ensure that prisoners are held only in officially recognized places of detention and that accurate information about their arrest and whereabouts is made available immediately to relatives, lawyers and the courts. Effective judicial remedies should be available to enable relatives and lawyers to find out immediately where a prisoner is held and under what authority and to ensure the prisoner's safety.

4. Provide safeguards during detention and interrogation

All prisoners should be immediately informed of their rights. These include the right to lodge complaints about their treatment and to have a judge rule without delay on the lawfulness of their detention. Judges should investigate any evidence of torture and order release if the detention is unlawful. A lawyer should be present during interrogations. Governments should ensure that conditions of detention conform to international standards for the treatment of prisoners and take into account the needs of members of particularly vulnerable groups. The authorities responsible for detention should be separate from those in charge of interrogation. There should be regular, independent, unannounced and unrestricted visits of inspection to all places of detention.

5. Prohibit torture in law

Governments should adopt laws for the prohibition and prevention of torture incorporating the main elements of the UN Convention against Torture and Other Cruel, Inhuman or Degrading Treatment or Punishment (Convention against Torture) and other relevant international standards. All judicial and administrative corporal punishments should be abolished. The prohibition of torture and the essential safeguards for its prevention must not be suspended under any circumstances, including states of war or other public emergency.

6. Investigate

All complaints and reports of torture should be promptly, impartially and effectively investigated by a body independent of the alleged perpetrators. The methods and findings of such investigations should be made public. Officials suspected of committing torture should be suspended from active duty during the investigation. Complainants, witnesses and others at risk should be protected from intimidation and reprisals.

7. Prosecute

Those responsible for torture must be brought to justice. This principle should apply wherever alleged torturers happen to be, whatever their nationality or position, regardless of where the crime was committed and the nationality of the victims, and no matter how much time has elapsed since the commission of the crime. Governments must exercise universal jurisdiction over alleged torturers or extradite them, and cooperate with each other in such criminal proceedings. Trials must be fair. An order from a superior officer must never be accepted as a justification for torture.

8. No use of statements extracted under torture

Governments should ensure that statements and other evidence obtained through torture may not be invoked in any proceedings, except against a person accused of torture.

9. Provide effective training

It should be made clear during the training of all officials involved in the custody, interrogation or medical care of prisoners that torture is a criminal act. Officials should be instructed that they have the right and duty to refuse to obey any order to torture.

10. Provide reparation

Victims of torture and their dependants should be entitled to obtain prompt reparation from the state including restitution, fair and adequate financial compensation and appropriate medical care and rehabilitation.

11. Ratify international treaties

All governments should ratify without reservations international treaties containing safeguards against torture, including the UN Convention against Torture with declarations providing for individual and inter-state complaints. Governments should comply with the recommendations of international bodies and experts on the prevention of torture.

12. Exercise international responsibility

Governments should use all available channels to intercede with the governments of countries where torture is reported. They should ensure that transfers of training and equipment for military, security or police use do not facilitate torture. Governments must not forcibly return a person to a country where he or she risks being tortured.

This 12-Point Program was adopted by Amnesty International in October 2000 as a program of measures to prevent the torture and ill-treatment of people who are in governmental custody or otherwise in the hands of agents of the state. Amnesty International holds governments to their international obligations to prevent and punish torture, whether committed by agents of the state or by other individuals. Amnesty International also opposes torture by armed political groups.

ENDNOTES

1   The Children's Convention has been ratified by every country in the world, except the United States of America and the collapsed state of Somalia.

2   These include, but are not limited to, the UN Declaration on the Rights of the Child (1959); the UN Standard Minimum Rules for the Administration of Juvenile Justice (Beijing Rules) (1985); the UN Rules for the Protection of Juveniles Deprived of their Liberty (1990); the UN Guidelines for the Prevention of Juvenile Delinquency (The Riyadh Guidelines) (1996); the International Covenant on Civil and Political Rights (ICCPR) (1966); and the four Geneva Conventions of 1949 and their Protocols.

3   The UN Standard Minimum Rules for the Administration of Juvenile Justice, 1985, usually referred to as "The Beijing Rules".

4   Activism, Politics and the Punishment of Children, by Pamela Reynolds in *Childhood Abused: Protecting Children against Torture, Cruel, Inhuman and Degrading Treatment and Punishment*, edited by Geraldine Van Bueren, Ashgate, 1998, p. 54.

5   Beijing Rules, Rule 4. The Committee on the Rights of the Child has not pronounced on a minimum age, but regularly registers concern about countries where the legal age of criminal responsibility is very low, i.e., under 10. See, for example, CRC/C/15/Add.96, p. 15.

6   About 80 prisoners are on death row in 16 US states for crimes committed when they were 16 or 17 years old. The imposition of the death penalty on child offenders is prohibited by international law. AI believes that the death penalty is the ultimate cruel, inhuman and degrading punishment and violates the right to life. The execution itself causes extreme suffering, and prisoners on death row are also forced to contemplate, day after day, the end of their lives at the hands of the state.

7   In their 1958 Commentary on the Fourth Geneva Convention, the International Committee of the Red Cross stated that: "A person who has not reached the age of eighteen years is not fully capable of sound judgement, does not always realize the significance of his actions and often acts under the influence of others, if not under constraint."

8   In the case of armed political groups engaged in armed conflict, the protection from torture is derived mainly from international humanitarian law (IHL). Common Article 3 of the Geneva Conventions prohibits absolutely the torture or cruel treatment of all persons. Article 4.3 of the Protocol Additional to the Geneva Conventions... and relating to the Protection of Victims of Non-International Armed Conflicts (Protocol II) also stipulates that children under 15 are entitled to special protection even if they are taking active part in hostilities.

9   See note to Principle 6 in the UN Body of Principles for the Protection of All Persons under Any Form of Detention or Imprisonment (1988), which says: The term "cruel, inhuman or degrading treatment or punishment" should be interpreted so as to extend the widest possible protection against abuses, whether physical or mental, including the holding of a detained or imprisoned person in conditions which deprive him, temporarily or permanently of the use of any of his natural senses, such as sight or hearing, or of his awareness of place and the passing of time.

10 Article 7(2)(e) of the Rome Statute of the International Criminal Court.

11 The draft Elements of Crimes adopted by the Preparatory Commission for the International Criminal Court, which are designed to assist the Court in the interpetation of the Statute, further defines these two crimes. The Assembly of States Parties will adopt the final text when the Statute enters into force.

12 The American Convention on Human Rights and the European Convention for the Protection of Human Rights and Fundamental Freedoms, respectively. There are a number of other relevant regional standards which these two bodies can also take into account, including: the Inter-American Convention to Prevent and Punish Torture; the American Declaration of the Rights and Duties of Man; the Inter-American Convention on the Forced

Disappearance of Persons, 1994; and the European Convention for the Prevention of Torture and Inhuman or Degrading Treatment or Punishment.

13 In its commentary on a report on Norway, the Committee on the Right of the Child stated: "The Committee would like to suggest that the State party consider in its legislation the implications of article 37 (a) of the Convention on the Rights of the Child and, in this connection, that it also pay attention to the definition of torture provided for in Article 1 of the Convention against Torture and Other Cruel, Inhuman or Degrading Treatment or Punishment, to which Norway is also a party." CRC/C/15/Add.23., para 15.

14 Article 43(2) of the Children's Convention. An amendment raising the number of members to 18 has been ratified by about 50 state parties; another 70 ratifications will bring it into effect.

15 The Committee against Torture is a body of 10 experts established by the UN Convention against Torture. It can also consider complaints by one state against another, and can act upon receiving reliable information that torture is being practised systematically, including by undertaking a visit to the state concerned.

16 Ratifications figure as of September 2000. However, the Special Rapporteur on torture also investigates, comments on and makes recommendations on torture and ill-treatment in countries which are not states parties to the Convention against Torture.

17 The current Special Rapporteur is Nigel S. Rodley of the UK. Nigel Rodley was appointed Special Rapporteur in 1993. In 1998, his mandate was extended for three years by the Commission on Human Rights (resolution 1998/38).

18 The Human Rights Committee, in its General Comment 20, states: "In the Committee's view, moreover, the prohibition must extend to corporal punishment, including excessive chastisement ordered as punishment for a crime or as an educative or disciplinary measure. It is appropriate to emphasize in this regard that article 7 protects, in particular, children, pupils and patients in teaching and medical institutions."

19 Eric Sottas, "A Non-Governmental Organization Perspective of the United Nations' Approach to Children and Torture", in *Childhood Abused*, op cit, p 146.

20 *Innocenti Digest*, number 2, Children and Violence, UNICEF International Child Development Center, Florence, Italy. Children are also more likely to be murdered at home: about 60 per cent of all child murders are carried out by parents, and a further 27 per cent by other relatives.

21 Some child rights specialists have argued that domestic violence against children could fall within the human rights legal framework because the public/private dichotomy which applies to other human rights does not operate the same way where a child is concerned. The child is not autonomous like the adult, but is under the legal authority of the parent, in a manner analogous to the subordination of the adult to the state. For all practical purposes, however, the blanket prohibition on violence against children in the Children's Convention makes it a largely academic argument.

22 See comments by the Special Rapporteur on torture at E/CN.4/1997/7.

23 Rule 17.3.

24 Rule 67.

25 UN Commission on Human Rights Resolution 2000/43.

26 E/CN.4/2000/9 /Add.4 Report of the Special Rapporteur on torture: visit to Kenya, 1/03/00, paras 55-56. In July 2000, the government of Kenya announced that a ban on caning, first announced in 1996, would be enforced.

27 In Costello-Roberts v. United Kingdom, 1993, the European Court of Human Rights ruled that a case in which a school headmaster had whacked a seven-year-old boy three times on the buttocks with a slipper did not rise to the level of severity necessary to constitute a violation of human rights norms, including Article 3 of the European Convention on Human Rights.

28 See CRC/C/34.

29 Children's Convention articles 19 and 28.

30 Summary record of 176th meeting, CRC/C/SR.176, Oct 1994, para 46. In questioning the UK government about their periodic report, Thomas Hammarberg, a member of the Committee, noted that difficulties arose whenever a "reasonable" level of corporal punishment was permitted under a state's internal law. "To draw an analogy," he pointed out, "no one would argue that a 'reasonable' level of wife-beating should be permitted." The notion of a "permissible" level of corporal punishment, he concluded, was thus best avoided. CRC/C/SR.205 , 30 January 1995, paras 61-63.

31 See, for example, E/CN.4/1996/35, para 10.

32 "Psychosocial assessment of displaced children exposed to war-related violence in Sierra Leone", Plan International, February 2000.

33 See for example, "Psychosocial assessment of displaced children exposed to war-related violence in Sierra Leone", Plan International, February 2000; "Helping Children Cope with the Stresses of War", UNICEF, 1993; "Children: Noble Causes or Worthy Citizens", UNICEF, 1997; "In the Firing Line: War and Children's Rights", AIUK, 1999; Childhood Abused: Protecting Children against Torture, Cruel, Inhuman and Degrading Treatment and Punishment", edited by Geraldine Van Bueren, Ashgate, 1998.

34 Mona Macksoud, "Helping Children Cope with the Stresses of War," UNICEF, 1993.

35 Ibid, p 40.

36 Ibid, p 43.

37 Edith Montgomery, "Children Exposed to War, Torture and Other Organized Violence — Developmental Consequences", in Childhood Abused, op. cit., p 189.

38 Mona Macksoud, op. cit., pp 38-48.

39 Dora Black and Martin Newman, "The Effects on Children of Witnessing Violence Perpetrated against their Parents or Siblings", in Childhood Abused, op. cit., pp 205-222.

40 Adult caregivers who are interviewed about their child's symptoms of post-traumatic stress disorder consistently underestimate the objective effects of traumatic stress in children. Dyregrov and Raundalen, 1994, as reported in Plan International's Sierra Leone report, op. cit.

41 Jacobo Timerman, "Prisoner without a name, cell without a number", London 1981.

42 Interviews with about 30 Palestinian boys in 1989-1990. See also M Basoglu et al, "Psychological preparedness for trauma as a protective factor in survivors of torture", Psychological Medicine, 1997, 1421-1433.

43 Childhood Abused, op. cit., p 44.

44 Edith Montgomery, "Children Exposed to War, Torture and other organised violence — developmental consequences", in Childhood Abused, p 190. She is the Chief Psychologist at the Rehabilitation and Research Centre for Torture Victims in Denmark.

45 Statistics are bound to be unreliable for comparative purposes, as definitions of what constitutes "mental illness" vary from country to country and even within them. In the USA, for instance, estimates suggest that the percentage of juveniles incarcerated who have some kind of recognizable mental disorder could be up to 70 per cent, with some 20 per cent having very serious mental problems.

46 UN Declaration on the Rights of Mentally Retarded Persons, 1971; principles for the protection of persons with mental illness. Adopted by GA resolution 46/119 of 17 Dec 1991.

47 According to the UN Rules for the Protection of Juveniles Deprived of their Liberty, all juveniles are entitled to an examination by a physician immediately on admission to detention, which should identify "any physical or mental condition requiring medical attention" (Rule 50); those suffering mental illness have the right to treatment in a specialized institution, and to appropriate care after release (Rule 53).

48 Reported in *Article 40*, a publication of the Children's Rights Project, University of the Western Cape, August 1999.

49 Articles 12 and 13, Convention against Torture.

50 The absence of solid documentation to support and substantiate allegations by torture victims allows governments to deny the truth and evade their responsibilities. The Manual on Effective Investigation and Documentation of Torture and Other Cruel, Inhuman or Degrading Treatment or Punishment, known as the Istanbul Protocol, adopted in 1999, provides guidelines on how to assess and document medical evidence of torture. The Istanbul Protocol also outlines minimum standards which states should meet when they investigate complaints of torture. The Istanbul Protocol gives guidance to NGOs in their anti-torture work, and sets standards by which to assess official investigations.

51 For further information see *Sierra Leone: Rape and other forms of sexual violence against girls and women*, 29 June 2000, AI Index: AFR 51/35/00.

52 A pseudonym

53 E/CN.4/1998/38/Add.1.

54 E/CN.4/1998/38/Add.1.

55 ECN.4/2000/9, para 953.

56 E/CN.4/2000/9, para 538.

57 All of the names used here are pseudonyms. E/CN.4/1999/61 para 153.

58 Giving a keynote speech on 27 March 2000 at a meeting of the Organization for Security and Co-operation in Europe, the UN Special Rapporteur on torture stated that it was not difficult to identify what preventative measures could be taken to make substantial inroads into the bulk of the problem of torture. One was to keep to an absolute minimum the period during which detainees do not have access to the outside world. The other was to ensure independent supervision, by a body having an automatic right of access to any place of deprivation of liberty, especially police stations, and with the power to report publicly on its findings.

59 Robert Fisk, "At Khiam Jail: Inside a torturers' den, manacles lie abandoned", *Independent* newspaper, 25 May 2000, page 3.

60 E/CN.4/1998/38/Add.1.

61 Statistics provided by the Coalition to Stop the Use of Child Soldiers.

62 The Special Representative of the UN Secretary-General for Children and Armed Conflict said in September 1999 that "more than 10,000 children have been serving as child soldiers in various fighting groups." UNICEF estimates of the number of child soldiers were lower, at around 5,000, but with at least another 5,000 children being used by opposition forces to carry goods, cook and provide sexual services.

63 For further information on child combatants, see "Sierra Leone: Childhood — a casualty of conflict", 31 August 2000, AI Index AFR 51/69/00.

64 Pseudonym

65 Pseudonym

66 Article 3 of the Optional Protocol sets the minimum age for voluntary recruitment at 16, provided that safeguards are in place to ensure that recruitment is truly voluntary. Article 1 obliges states parties to take all feasible measures to ensure that children under 18 do not take a direct part in hostilities.

67 Coalition to Stop the Use of Child Soldiers, statement at May 2000 conference in Nepal.

68 Her full name is known to AI but has been withheld at the request of her lawyers.

69 *Prison Bound: the denial of juvenile justice in Pakistan*, Human Rights Watch, 1999.

70 Ibid, pp 20-21.

71 E/CN.4/1999/61, para 190.

72 Didier is a pseudonym. The boy's real name is known to AI but has been withheld on request.

73 "Nobody's Children": Jamaican Children in Police Detention and Government Institution, Human Rights Watch, 1999.

74 Juvenile Injustice, Police Abuse and Detention of Street Children in Kenya, Human Rights Watch, 1997, p 21.

75 Inter-American Commission Press Release No. 23/99: Commission ends on-site visit to Paraguay, 30 July 1999.

76 Diario ABC 15 February 2000 Murió otro quemado del Panchito López en la madrugada de ayer.

77 In 1997, Paraguay reported to the Committee on the Rights of the Child that there were 239 boys in Panchito López, only six of whom (3%) had been convicted of any crime. The case filed by the Fundación Tekojoja and CEJIL in 1996 said there were about 300 minors detained there, while Senator Luis Alberto Mauro, a member of the government's Human Rights Commission, made reference in late February 2000 to the "270" minors then being held.

78 Diario ABC, 12/2/00, Dos muertos y 28 heridos en incendio en "Panchito". It was also suggested that the boys were protesting against the failure of the system to process their cases.

79 Prison Bound: The denial of juvenile justice in Pakistan, Human Rights Watch, 1999, p 41.

80 HM Chief Inspector of Prisons, Report of an unannounced Full Inspection, 26 March 1999.

81 Promises Broken: An Assessment of Children's Rights on the 10th Anniversary of the Convention on the Rights of the Child, Human Rights Watch, November 1999.

82 Death by Default: A study of fatal neglect in China's state orphanages, Human Rights Watch, January 1996.

83 Abandoned to the State: Cruelty and Neglect in Russian Orphanages, Human Rights Watch, December 1998.

WHAT YOU CAN DO

- Join our campaign — **Take a step to stamp out torture**
  You can help stamp out torture. Add your voice to Amnesty
  International's campaign. Help us to make a difference. Contact
  your national office of Amnesty International and ask for
  information about how to join the campaign, including information
  on how to take action on some of the specific cases featured in this
  report.
- Become a member of Amnesty International and other local and
  international human rights organization which fight torture
- Make a donation to support Amnesty International's work
- Tell friends and family about the campaign and ask them to join too

Campaigning Online

The website **www.stoptorture.org** allows visitors to access AI's
information about torture. It will also offer the opportunity to appeal
on behalf of individuals at risk of being tortured. Those registering onto
the site will receive urgent e-mail messages alerting them to take
action during the campaign.

- Register to take action against torture at **www.stoptorture.org**

**For more information on Amnesty International's work,
particularly in the United States and Canada, or a listing
of AI publications with dollar prices, visit www.amnestyusa.org
or write to:**

USA: Amnesty International USA Publications,
   322 Eighth Ave,
   New York NY 10001

Canada:Amnesty International, Canadian Section
   (English speaking)
   214 Montreal Road #401,
   Vanier, Ontario K1L 1A4

   Amniste Internationale, Section Canadienne
   (Francophone)
   6250 boulevard Monk,
   Montreal, Quebec H4E 3H7